VIEW TO THE SOUTHEAST

Books by Santha Rama Rau

GIFTS OF PASSAGE

MY RUSSIAN JOURNEY

VIEW TO THE SOUTHEAST

REMEMBER THE HOUSE

THIS IS INDIA

EAST OF HOME

HOME TO INDIA

VIEW TO THE SOUTHEAST

by Santha Rama Rau

HARPER & ROW, PUBLISHERS

NEW YORK, EVANSTON, AND LONDON

to

RUTH CAMM

with affection

Acknowledgments

Most of the material in this book appeared first in *Holiday* as articles in the magazine's series "The New World of Asia." I would like to express my thanks to the editors of *Holiday* for permission to reprint those articles, and particularly to Harry Sions for his meticulous and tactful editing.

CONTENTS

xi

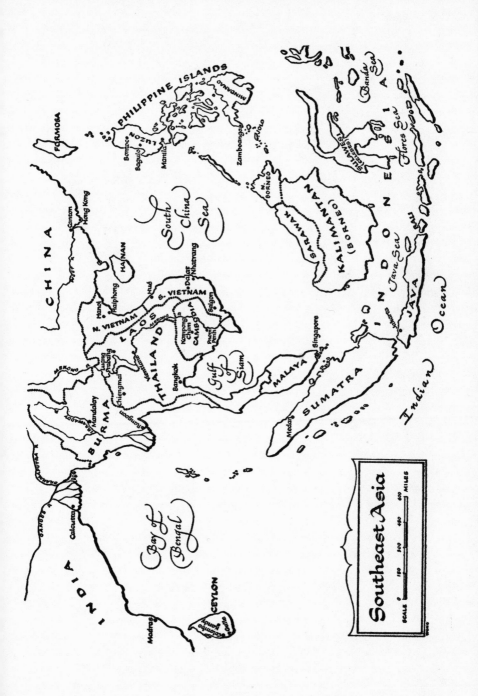

{ VIEW TO THE SOUTHEAST }

SOUTHEAST ASIA, WHICH IS PROBABLY MORE accurately described as Central-South Asia, is that stretch of the earth's surface that extends from the eastern borders of India across the Asian mainland to the Chinese frontier and the far coast of Indo-China. It includes the islands that are scattered in a graceful curve across the equator from Ceylon through Indonesia and north to the Philippines. It is one of the most complex, diverse, charming, distressing, surprising areas in the world. It is also virtually unexplored by people who travel for pleasure. A few of its more famous sights are known to tourists—Bali, say, or Angkor—but for the most part it remains remote, mysterious and far more obscure than the articulate, troublesome or powerful nations of Asia that surround it. I suppose a relatively small number of Americans would be able to tell you with confidence just where Laos is—although Laos is of a comparable size to England; I dare say they might have difficulty remembering the capital of Indonesia—although Indonesia is the third-biggest democracy in the world. They would even have trouble finding books to inform them in a general way about Southeast Asia, for apart from a few scholarly treatises about specific places, or political and economic analyses of certain countries or problems, there is very little written with a nontechnical approach in English about the area as a whole.

This book is an account of a journey through Southeast Asia

3

that lasted something over a year, and on which I was accompanied by my husband, Faubion Bowers, our small son and Mrs. Ruth Camm. My husband was completing his book, *Theatre in the East*, a survey of dance and drama forms in Asia, and wanted to bring his earlier researches up to date—this, of course, explains the rather overemphatic place theatrical performances assumed in our travels. I was writing articles for various American magazines. Although these were the logical reasons for our travels, looking back at that year now, the major purpose seems to have been simply that we enjoy that part of the world and had, during earlier visits, seen enough of it to want to explore it a little further. Consequently, this book is in no sense a profound or comprehensive report on Southeast Asia (though such a report is badly needed); it is intended only to fill, in a very modest and incomplete way, the gap between the serious, detailed literature of the specialists and the occasional tourist pamphlet of such Southeast Asian countries as have tourist bureaus.

I have tried to give, for the casual traveler in Southeast Asia, some idea of the general conditions he can expect, something of the background of the people and places he may see, some of the amusements, activities or short trips that I particularly enjoyed. Naturally, we each pursued our particular interests or pleasures during our journey, so this book reflects very little more than a personal view of what was, for me, an unusually interesting year. If there is any deeper significance to be drawn from all this, it is, perhaps, simply that in dealing with countries, as with anything else, you can't really understand them unless you also like them—and that does give at least one extra value to the pursuit of pleasure.

Southeast Asia, even more than the United States, deserves to be called a melting pot. Racially the stock is mostly Malay, but along the Chinese borders and certainly in Northern Vietnam the Chinese infiltration has been so heavy that the racial type appears to be virtually Mongolian. Besides this, in every major Southeast Asian city there is a large, thriving, active community of semipermanent Chinese exiles—the "overseas Chinese"—who often have not renounced their original nationality, sometimes send their sons back to China for their education, occasionally retire to China in their old age, but leave behind the younger members of their family to live and work in the foreign country.

Even the southern and central parts of Southeast Asia are not a racially homogeneous group. You can find Melanesians in New Guinea (which by national claim, if not by geography, is counted as part of Southeast Asia). In central Luzon or in Borneo you will come upon the various aboriginal tribes of Igorots, Ifugaos or Dyaks—most of them reformed head-hunters, although this is an appellation the people would like to forget. Along the outer borders of Burma you can see the dozens of different hill tribes, each with its special racial and cultural characteristics. And as you move westward toward India you cannot help noticing the strong Indian admixture that centuries of contact have brought to the Burmese and the people of Ceylon. Here the straight hair, the small nose, the characteristic fold in the upper eyelid—all typical of Mongolian racial types—give way to curly hair, more prominent features, a darker skin and, finally, the particular structure of the eye which is common to all Caucasians.

This meeting and mingling of races is even more strongly reflected in the culture of Southeast Asia, for it is here that the two great civilizations of Asia, the Indian and the Chinese, came up against each other. Sometimes they clashed with a violence that led to warfare, as for instance in the Chinese attacks on the ancient empire of Cambodia; sometimes they met more gently

5

and survived together, producing curious anomalies of language, art, dress or food. In Bangkok, for example, you can stay in a hotel with the implacably Sanskrit name of Suryanond or Ratnacosin, can listen to the Siamese speaking a tonal language strongly related to Chinese, and yet see that same language written in a script that derives from the Indian *devanagari* of curves and curlycues written beneath the line instead of on the line. You can eat typically Siamese food only to find that it has much of the flavor, style and character of Chinese food, yet it must include the chilis and spices that one associates with Indian cuisine. In South Vietnam you can see the curving roofs, the lacquered pillars, the tiles and dragons that are characteristic of Chinese architecture and decoration, close beside the ruins of the stone temples and elaborate carvings of ancient Hinduism.

The religious history of this relatively small area is possibly the most remarkable and complicated of any in the world. Southeast Asia contains all the major religions and a number of minor ones. The Chinese influences in Northern Vietnam have produced a strong bias toward Confucianism and Taoism; in the other countries of Indo-China and in Thailand, Malaya, Burma and Ceylon, Buddhism is the national religion although there still remain traces of their earlier conversion to Hinduism and of their still earlier forms of animism and spirit worship. In Burma, for example, in a corner of the courtyard surrounding a conventional Buddhist temple you may easily see a separate small shrine dedicated to the *nats*—the sprites and spirits of the earth and air or of history. Or you may learn that in Cambodia, where the king, like the rest of his subjects, is Buddhist, there are still three Brahmin priests permanently retained at court to perform the most traditional ceremonies.

In Indonesia this overlay of one religion on another is even

6

more strikingly illustrated. Here the converting wave of Islam swept down from the Arab countries through India to reach the islands. Indonesia is now predominantly Muslim, but the previous layer of Hindu culture still shows up in names, in architecture and other arts, in speech and in customs. You will often see an entirely Muslim audience watching, enthralled, one of the famous Indonesian shadow plays that tell stories from the great, intimately familiar legends of Hindu mythology—the Ramayana and the Mahabharata—as inescapably a part of Muslim Indonesia's tradition as they are of Hindu India's.

However, in Indonesia you also find the only Hindu country in the world outside India itself. The island of Bali, which inexplicably escaped the Islamic conversion and in the fourteenth century gave shelter to the great Hindu raja from Java, Madjapahit, still retains its Hinduism. The forms may be a bit different and modified, but the feeling is just about as intense as it is in the homeland of India.

Southeast Asia has, as well, the only predominantly Christian country in all Asia; the Philippine Islands, converted in the fifteenth century by the Spaniards, have largely retained their Catholicism although some of the southern islands came within the scope of the Islamic invasions. In these, particularly in Jolo and the Sulu Islands, the converted Muslims live by a particularly militant form of their religion, one that allowed a "bandit" ruler like Kamlon of the island of Jolo to demand the allegiance of fellow Muslims in a fight against the Philippine government that lasted for years, involved thousands of Philippine troops, and was intended to set up an independent Muslim government for the islands. There too, the baffling but terrifying tradition of "amok" (practically unknown in other Muslim countries) still flourishes. It means that any Muslim who feels his *amour-propre* in any way

7

offended—this may be caused by a disappointment in love or merely by an insulting look in the eye of a stranger—can go amok, killing anyone in sight until he himself is killed. There is a Spanish word for this in the Philippine Islands, *juramentado*— a sworn one.

In Southeast Asia you can still find evidences of some of the most ancient religions in history. Off the coast of Sumatra, on an island called Nias, there remains one of the world's extremely few examples of Stone Age culture. The religious rites, performed at huge stone altars, require of the Nias men astonishing feats of high-jumping as part of the traditional ritual. In central Java there is an isolated community that lives on the side of a volcano. This tribe was left untouched by both the Hindu and the Muslim conversions, and still retains its protohistoric worship of the terrible and powerful volcano which provides a livelihood (on its fertile lower slopes), but can just as easily send a sudden and meaningless annihilation, and must, therefore, be pacified with living sacrifices of goats, pigs and oxen that are pushed down the crater to their terrifying and unwilling death.

Equally, in Southeast Asia, some of the newest religions in the world have found themselves a healthy soil and plenty of followers. Perhaps the most remarkable of these is the Cao Dai movement of Vietnam, which has its own elaborate religious hierarchy headed by a Pope, supported by bishops and priests and thousands of devotees. It has, besides, its own most original roster of saints, which includes among many others Benjamin Franklin, Victor Hugo and Queen Elizabeth II. On the outskirts of Saigon you can see the enormous and lavish cathedral where Cao Dai services are held; on the Saigon streets you will often watch processions of Cao Dai followers with their distinctive blue and yellow satin emblems, carrying banners emblazoned with the Cao Dai mystic symbols, all in celebration of special Cao Dai festivals or saints' days. You will also quickly learn that the Cao Dai-ists have considerable political influence and a police force that amounts to a private army and was a major political factor until very recently.

The reason for this extraordinary hodgepodge of religions, cultures and races concentrated in Southeast Asia is essentially an economic one. This stretch of mountains, plains and islands is the richest region in Asia and has, inevitably, attracted the predatory attention of its bigger, but more impoverished neighbors as well as the greedy eyes of many Western powers. The climate of Southeast Asia is uniformly and lushly tropical. Crops, flowers, trees grow with the minimum of attention. In some parts agricultural communities raise as many as four rice crops each year. Fruit and vegetables are plentiful the whole year round. Rivers, lakes and the countless island coasts provide fish. A heavy meat diet is in any case unnecessary in a climate where the temperature never goes much above ninety and never sinks much below seventy. In contrast with India, China or Japan, Southeast Asia has practically no population pressures. The island of Java and the coastal strip of northern Vietnam are perhaps the only exceptions. For centuries past and even to the present day, the region has been, to its Asian neighbors, the "Great Rice Bowl" of Asia. For Western powers it had a more exotic attraction —here in Southeast Asia were the fabulous Spice Islands; here, too, was the source of teak and ivory, sandalwood and rare perfumes, of silks, cinnamon, pearls, and before the exploration and settlement of Africa, the world's richest store of gold and precious stones.

It was only to be expected that Southeast Asia should turn out to be the most intensively colonized area in the world, with a history of conquest and subjugation unequaled in any other continent. For, in the sixteenth and seventeenth centuries vast fortunes could be made on one shipload of pepper. Fleets of pirates, privateers, legitimate traders battled each other and the local populations to capture the spice trade. Heroes and explorers like Magellan and Vasco da Gama died in attempts to establish their country's right to the unimagined wealth of Southeast Asia. The British, French, Dutch, Portuguese and Spanish were all involved in the rancorous, turbulent history of Southeast Asia's colonization, but actually they were latecomers to the imperialist scene.

For centuries before the Western nations discovered Southeast Asia, China had been invading, raiding, conquering from the east and north. The invincible armies of Kublai Khan had reached as far as Burma, and at one time every country in Southeast Asia paid tribute to the distant, intimidating force of the Chinese emperor. Even before recorded history the mainland of Southeast Asia had been fought over, and even now you find reminders of those centuries of battles in some of the names of towns and countries. Siemreap, for instance, the small town where you stay when you go to visit the Angkor ruins, means "the defeat of Siam." The "viet" of Vietnam is a Chinese word designating the conquered people of the southern peninsula. When, in the ninth century, China annexed Vietnam by the force of what were then the most massive armies known, they called it "Annam" or "The Pacified Southern Country," and that name too recurs constantly in Indo-China. It was supposed to remind the Viets of their subjugation, but the Viets would, from time to time, revolt against their Chinese conquerors and call themselves (still borrowing from the Chinese) "Dai Viet" or "The Great Viet Country." But these periods of Vietnamese self-rule were usually pretty brief, and the Chinese kept returning and reapplying the old humiliating name Annam.

While the force of this immense civilization was bearing down on Southeast Asia from the north and east, India, from the west, began its great period of cultural and commercial expansion. From the third to the thirteenth centuries (and possibly even earlier, from the time of Emperor Asoka) the Indian influence spread through the mainland and from there continued into the islands. Priests, scholars, traders, artists, artisans and in some cases soldiers flooded Southeast Asia, entirely changing the cultural face of the region, leaving a vast residue of art, legend and habit. The Indians differed in one important way from the Chinese in their expansion: although they set up great empires and powerful kingdoms, the Indians that embarked on this "colonization" did not behave like other empire builders; they didn't return the wealth of these foreign countries to their own homeland. They didn't exact tribute for India or make their cultural or political conquests in India's name. Most often, in fact, they lost their own allegiance to their home country and settled down as citizens of whatever area of Southeast Asia they had reached. So, for instance, they established the royal line of the vital kingdom of Cambodia or the far-flung empire of Sri Vijaya, but after that each nation retained its sovereignty and its identity entirely separate from India. It might borrow its art, religion or way of life from India, but it remained an independent nation—until it was again defeated by a neighbor or an invading Western power.

Even the Japanese, who, until a hundred years ago, had been famous for their rigid isolationism, made advances toward Southeast Asia. Coxinga, the famous "pirate" and ruler, for example, sent out envoys from his headquarters in Formosa demanding the immediate surrender of the Philippines. Besides this, in the sixteenth century, rather mysterious bands of Japanese soldiers were known to exist in many scattered places on the mainland. Apparently they became professional mercenaries and fought in any army that hired them, and in old accounts of this period one can learn that the Japanese soldiers were the best fighters in—say—the Burmese army.

The best-known period of colonization in Southeast Asia's troubled history begins, of course, with the arrival of the European adventurers and explorers in the fourteenth and fifteenth centuries. At first there were only isolated raids and battles, short, indecisive conquests of an island or a small town. A few trading posts were set up, a few heavily fortified stockades to guard a tentative, shifting hold on a continent. These turned into "companies," often with royal charters. By the sixteenth and seventeenth centuries the first Western colonies in Asia were firmly established—the Portuguese in Ceylon, the Dutch in Indonesia, the Spanish in the Philippines.

With the exception of Thailand, which managed by an extraordinary political canniness and historical accident to retain its independence, every country of Southeast Asia was conquered by one or another of the European nations and remained a colony until the last World War. The Dutch defeated the Portuguese in Ceylon and added that island, too, to their enormous island empire. The British, in turn, defeated the Dutch and took over the rule of Ceylon. Later, they moved further east to capture Burma and Malaya and the scattered islands in the Indian Ocean, the Andamans and the Nicobars, and part of the Indonesian island of Borneo. More recently still, the French conquered Indo-China, which included North and South Vietnam, Cambodia and Laos.

And only sixty years ago the Americans fought the Spaniards for control of the Philippines.

Although in all these years, in virtually every colony, there were innumerable independence movements, uprisings, sometimes outright revolution, in every case these attempts were suppressed, sometimes by a modification of colonial rule, and sometimes simply by superior force. During the recent World War, the last of Southeast Asia's colonizers, Japan, at last turned its full imperialistic attention on the rich and useful area between the enemy country of China and the semi-hostile nation of India. For the first time the people of Southeast Asia saw the "white man" defeated by a fellow Asian nation, and at first, if there was not active assistance to the Japanese from the people of Southeast Asia, at least there was a passive acceptance of what might have seemed, at the time, like a liberation from colonial rule.

Soon after the war when I was in Indo-China, people would often remind me of the time, so fresh in their memory, when the French military leaders who had put up no fight against the Japanese could be seen drinking champagne in the best hotels with their Japanese counterparts. "And now," the story always used to end, "they expect us to take them back as colonial rulers as if nothing had happened." In fact, very soon after the Japanese occupation of Southeast Asia the people saw that they had only exchanged one colonialism for another. Underground movements began in most of the countries, and by the time the Allied armies regained Southeast Asia there were strong anti-Japanese guerrillas to assist them. Ironically, those Southeast Asian nationals found themselves rescuing their own colonial conquerors from the new colonial rule of the Japanese.

For most of Southeast Asia the war did not end in 1945. For a brief period after the defeat of the Japanese a number of the countries—Cambodia, Vietnam, Laos, Indonesia, Burma—set up independent governments to rule themselves now that they were, at last, free of foreign domination of any sort. These governments immediately came into conflict with the returning colonial powers. In some cases this crisis was handled swiftly and intelligently, most notably by the British, who granted independence to Burma and assisted the Burmese government in quelling its dissident elements, who also co-operated in the more gradual independence of Ceylon. In the Philippines, too, the long-promised independence from American rule was given a concrete reality. But in Indonesia it took five years of fighting from the independence armies before the United Nations pressure forced the Dutch to accept Indonesia's right to rule itself. In Indo-China the fighting continued until 1954 before some kind of settlement could be reached to establish independence there.

While the problem of "color" is sometimes grossly exaggerated and sometimes entirely ignored, still it is no use pretending that the slights, social insults, and the assumption of superiority that were part of the Western domination of Southeast Asia did not and do not still play a large part in the drive for independence and in the more recent uncommitted or nonalignment policies.

Meanwhile, in a couple of the countries the new governments were suddenly challenged by Communist-inspired uprisings, which hoped to win over the people at a moment of instability and confusion. Both in Burma and in the Philippines the new independent governments managed to cope with this added problem. But in the places where anticolonial fighting still continued —particularly in Malaya and in Indo-China—movements that had started out as assertions of nationalism began to find the further strength that they needed in Communist sympathy and support. In Malaya that conflict still continues. In Indo-China there is, at best, a temporary, nervous truce and an unsolved, complicated problem for the future.

With this restless, tragic, war-fraught history behind them, with their long experience of conquests, subjugation, colonial rule, cultural domination, it seems astonishing that Southeast Asians should have retained a special, charming character of their own, a distinctive gaiety, a love of life, a pleasantly humorous *laissez-faire*, a gentle flexibility. All these are aspects of a quality of character that the Indonesians call *alus* and admire very much, and if you should (as you can) translate *alus* as "soft," they will not contradict you, though you will have missed what they consider the essential virtue of the Southeast Asian character. The Southeast Asians can display violence, bitterness and bigotry, and have in their past, but—as far as one can generalize about a region of nearly 200 million people—their nature seems to me to be directed by these forces only in a very small degree. Gradually over the centuries they have managed to modify and adapt to their own particular temperament the religions, cultures and influences that have been forced on them by the rest of the world. If Bali, for instance, remains Hindu in its arts and religion, it is without the Indian philosophic intensity, without the Indian sense of mysticism, without the dour introspection of the Indian character. In Bali the Hindu tradition is far more lighthearted; there is a feeling for frivolity (oddly lacking in India), a warm, extroverted approach to the world, and the mystic attributes of Hinduism become transmuted, in Bali, to the intellectually simpler concept of magic.

In the same way the Buddhism of the Southeast Asian mainland would never produce the sophisticated subtleties of Japanese

15

Zen, or the elegant cynicism or the almost legalistically tabulated ethics of China. In Southeast Asia's Christianity the appeal of martyrdom, the sense of the value of suffering, or even of saintliness, is nowhere near as strong as it is in the countries of Christianity's origin and early growth. However, it is equally false to describe the Southeast Asians as "childlike," "simple," or part of what I think of as the "South Sea island dream." They are far more complex than that, and far more worthy of artistic respect.

It is true that in Southeast Asia you can find that idyllic island with crescent-shaped beaches of golden sand fringed with coconut palms, the friendly and beautiful natives, the remote and languorous atmosphere. The south coast of Ceylon appears to be very much like that, so does Bali, so do the Sulu Islands in the southern Philippines. But this conventionally romantic surface is just as untrue of the nature of the country as so many of those silly, but popularly accepted myths such as, "the Japanese are a nation of imitators," or "you can never tell what the Chinese are thinking." In fact, it is precisely the discrepancy between the "South Sea island dream" and the real character of the region that makes Southeast Asia such an enthralling and such an unexpectedly stimulating place in which to travel.

Artistically, Southeast Asia is enormously rewarding. The celebrated architecture and sculpture of Angkor are not the product of a delightfully primitive people. They do not belong to the quaint and colorful school of "native" art. On the contrary they are a profoundly moving expression of a highly developed nation, and are, besides, possibly the greatest single group of ruins in the world. Borobudur and Prambanan, both temples in Indonesia, and Polonnaruwa in Ceylon are smaller in scope but certainly of comparable quality. The inspiration for all these magnificent works of art came from India, but that is as irrelevant a comment on the artistic grasp and output of Southeast Asia as it would be to insist that the French were derivative because the Louvre was modeled on the styles of the Italian renaissance.

Together with their ancient heritage the countries of Southeast Asia continue to reach an internationally respected standard in their modern arts. Javanese and Balinese music and dancing are among the most expert and beautiful in the world, the current literary movement in the Philippines is increasingly impressive, the Burmese have a lively and flourishing theatre, each country has its particular excellence and all are products of rich and evolved civilizations. It is this rare and expressive combination of a vast and diverse heritage and a sympathetically appealing character that makes Southeast Asia particularly absorbing to me. It is never dull and heavy; neither is it shallow. The people are accessible, but not at the price of dignity and depth. The things to see, hear and do are infinitely varied and equally interesting. And finally, there is a sort of added bonus for any traveler in this area in the truly startling physical beauty of the people and their countryside. Whether you find yourself in the foothills of the Himalayas in northern Burma, the dramatic mountains and gorges of the Chinese borderland, the great emerald-green rice plains of central Thailand, the deep uncharted forests of Sumatra, or the bays and harbors of the island of Celebes—in fact, anywhere in Southeast Asia you will have that peculiarly pleasing experience of being surrounded by beautiful people with their lovely country as a permanent backdrop to everything you do.

Just before we started on the journey recorded in this book, we had been living in Japan; consequently we began our travels with the nearest Southeast Asian country, the Philippine Islands.

Although, for most of the region, this voyage from east to west rather reverses the actual flow of history and the expanding route of cultural influence, I am leaving the material on the various countries in the chronological order in which we visited them. We were not following historical trends, neither were we primarily concerned with deep researches into cultural manifestations. We were simply out to enjoy ourselves, and from that point of view we found Southeast Asia among the most rewarding places we have ever been, and our haphazard route perhaps reflects some part of that attitude.

As far as possible we tried to make our headquarters, in any country, outside the "westernized" centers of commerce and government. In Indonesia, for instance, we lived in the small hill town of Bogor rather than in the better-known and more comfortable city of Jakarta. We found that, although the basic necessities of life were always met, a number of luxuries were entirely absent—no hot water unless you yelled across the courtyard of the small Indonesian hotel to the kitchen quarters, and then one of the houseboys would come running with a small steaming pot of freshly boiled water with which you would manage somehow. No lights strong enough to read by at night. Springless beds, no carpets, the bare minimum of wooden furniture. Geese, chickens, stray dogs wandering onto your verandah with no one bothering to control them.

But we also discovered the joys of informal living in Indonesia, of having dozens of Indonesian children tearing about the courtyard with whom our own child played, communicating in some weird mixture of languages, gestures and intuition. We learned the special flavors of Indonesian food, explored the tiny restaurants in the village, stopped at roadside stands to buy the lumps of delicious spiced meats impaled on bamboo skewers. We shared the pleasure of any Indonesian guest at the hotel—or, indeed, of anyone in the village—who had decided to have a concert of an evening. We, ourselves, learned the technique of calling in the local musicians, a singer accompanied by a flute and a stringed instrument, or perhaps a whole orchestra, or even a storyteller chanting and acting out the old stories and legends. Then we would sit in the courtyard under the night sky, listening, and we would soon be joined by the other people in the hotel; the room boys would stand around between chores, all listening and occasionally applauding, and anyone passing on the street who heard the music would wander in and join the audience.

We became involved in local festivals, paid our small tribute to the dancing dragon that the Chinese brought around on New Year's Day, jostled with the crowd on Independence Day, watched the processions and flags and heard the shouted slogans of the demonstrators for West Irian's return to Indonesia. We fell into the relaxed pace of Indonesian life, learned to greet strangers, or talk to the vendors of fruit and vegetables who passed by the hotel. And that, in itself, led to further discoveries. We would ask, "What is the name of that fruit?" "Do you cook it or eat it raw?" and try for the first time the sweet-sour *sursac*, the consistency of custard with the faint flavor of almonds, or the penetratingly sweet and fragrant *mangis*, or the gelatinous *rambutan*. We were compelled to learn enough Indonesian to communicate, to order things, buy things, ask questions, and eventually simply to talk to friends. All this we felt would have taken far longer in a big city—or been missed entirely, replaced by the life of foreign clubs, American movies, European restaurants and night clubs, all the small fortresses that the foreigner builds against his homesickness.

For the same reasons and in the same way when we were in Laos, we preferred the unruffled atmosphere and faint, pervasive air of fantasy of Luang Prabang, the Laotian royal city, to the more familiar, but more pedestrian life of the French capital, Vientiane. In Ceylon we lived in the old southern port town of Galle, rather than the big, busy, modern capital of Colombo. I don't think that these preferences of ours gave us any profound understanding or insight into the countries we visited, but at least we felt in closer contact with their people and their life.

A couple of over-all experiences in our travels interested me particularly and I think are worth passing on to anyone visiting Southeast Asia. We found that traveling with a small child, far from being the worrisome bore we had half expected, turned out to be simple, comfortable, and in many cases a distinct advantage. The needs of children are, of course, understood everywhere, but in Southeast Asia there seems to be a specially flexible and accommodating attitude to children, and, by extension, to their parents. We made a number of friends and acquaintances only because our son had approached some stranger's child in an airport, a park, a zoo, a bazaar. We were given some very good advice from people we met in this way—we learned, for instance, that we should give a child papaya in places where orange juice was unavailable. It was only later that we found out that papaya does, in fact, contain the same vitamins. We were told that one segment of jack fruit contains the same properties as an egg (it has the same protein content), that the way to check an attack of diarrhea is to keep a child on a diet of rice gruel, curds and mashed ripe bananas for a few days. We also received some rather surprising advice, such as: Don't let your child stay out in the sun too long, he will grow up stupid; or, Never let your child's stomach remain uncovered, he will certainly catch cold.

In Southeast Asia, as in the rest of the continent, it is considered perfectly all right to take your child with you wherever you go—to a friend's house for dinner, to the theatre, to a dance that may last all night. If he gets sleepy, you settle him down in any convenient place, on a cot in the next room, on a mat on the verandah, on your lap, on the ground beside you if the entertainment is in the open air. None of the adults consider this either a bother or an interruption. If, on the other hand, there are other children around (as there nearly always are) and your child is interested or excited or enjoying himself with his contemporaries, then he is permitted to stay up as long as he likes, and, in many of the entertainments of Southeast Asia, is even allowed to join in the performance, copying the actions of the actors or dancers, or taking the part of any animal that happens to figure in the story. Our child's experience of this system left him with a passionate delight in the theatre (which, unfortunately, he can seldom indulge in the West). It gave us some amusing moments, too. After he had seen a devil dance in Ceylon and watched with an awed fascination the rapid, whirling movements when the dancers hold a smoldering torch in one hand and a fistful of gunpowder in the other, occasionally flinging the powder onto the torch to make sheets of flame, our son would attempt to duplicate the dances with a bunch of twigs in one hand and talcum powder in the other. It kept us pretty short of talcum powder but seemed to give him a lot of pleasure.

The religious diversity of Southeast Asia impressed him in a different way. He had seen the celebrations that accompany the birthday of Lord Buddha, which involved lights and decorations in the streets, the shops and the private houses, and the exchange of presents, usually fruit and rice and cloth. He had also seen Lord Krishna's birthday celebrations—involving lights and decorations in the streets, the shops and the private houses, and the exchange of presents, usually sweets. When we returned to America he celebrated his first Christmas and found that Lord Jesus' birthday involved lights and decorations in the streets, the shops and the private houses, and the exchange of presents. He was rather torn in his affiliation between little Lord Jesus, whose birthday produced the most lavish presents, and little Lord Krishna, whose personality as a naughty child (stealing the butter, disobeying his mother, teasing the girls) appealed to him more strongly. Whatever he finally decides for himself, I like to think that he will always respect and have a sympathetic enjoyment of the religion of other people.

Another aspect of these journeyings struck me as interesting—perhaps even significant. The last time I had been in Southeast Asia I had been inquiring, a certain amount, into politics there. I had asked questions about "conditions," about the standard of living, about political affiliations. I had received a number of touchy, suspicious or resentful responses. Occasionally, I had run into a rigid unwillingness to give out any information at all. This time, when we were more concerned with amusing ourselves, I found no such wariness. The people who might have been careful about involving themselves in a political discussion were instantly communicative and enthusiastic about, say, their music. Sometimes I found those other, more alarming questions answered in unexpected ways. For instance, an acquaintance who would cautiously evade direct questions about the economic muddles of South Vietnam would cheerfully take you to see a Vietnamese play that dealt most frankly with the economic muddles of South Vietnam—and would gladly answer your requests for clarification of the play's theme. It has been said that art is mankind's most authentic record; it was more surprising to me to learn that it can also be most revealing about modern conditions in a country.

The surface life of Manila is gay and confident and friendly, but if you read the short stories of some of the young Filipino writers you will find the painful search for identity, the curious mixture of uncertainty and pride that, in the ordinary way, is the hidden part of the Filipino character. The Thais appear to accept with equanimity, even possibly with gratitude, the growing American influence in their country. Go to their racy, irreverent *likay* theatres (with an interpreter, of course) and between the plays about kings and queens there will be comic interludes with plenty of fast, satiric comment on present conditions in Thailand. Ask about classical dancing in Burma and you will suddenly see an almost fierce determination replace the normally easygoing approach of the Burmese, and you will learn that they felt their classical arts were deeply slighted during their colonial period. While there is little bitterness against their ex-rulers in other fields, it does appear in their nationalistic wish to re-establish their arts and language.

This whole business of "understanding" foreign countries and people is a relatively new idea among nations. In Asia, with very few exceptions, it dates really only since the last war. Before that Asia's relations with the West, and even with neighboring Asian countries, were usually on the basis of conqueror and conquered, or of a mutually useful and wary peace, or of some aspect of "a balance of power," or of plain ignorance. Nobody seemed to think that the thoughts, aspirations, fears, problems, culture of another country were worth "understanding" for their own sake or as an element in the establishment of world peace. That kind of study or travel was left to scholars and eccentrics. Now this motivation is becoming increasingly popular, and many more people seem able to accept the idea that "understanding" is a good thing to pursue, and indeed, in helping to prevent another world war, may even save our lives. So I think that for any traveler in Asia it is worth remembering that the arts and pleasures of a country are worth exploring—they are probably the quickest and most painless path to "understanding."

All these aspects of Southeast Asian countries seemed to me interesting and important during my last visit. But, of course, in that year, as in any other year of my life, the most memorable moments concerned the people we met who amused, or taught, or pleased, or befriended us, without whom, for their own sakes and as interpreters of their countries, traveling in Southeast Asia would have been no more than an exotic, but meaningless, adventure.

THE PHILIPPINES

a tumultuous mixture

LONG, LONG AGO, SAYS AN OLD PHILIPPINE legend, a bluebird was flying between the sky and the sea. It had been flying for thousands of years, and it had become very tired. To get some rest it provoked a quarrel between the sky and the sea. The quarrel became a fight; the sea threw water at the sky, the sky threw meteors into the sea. Those meteors, scattered in a graceful, haphazard pattern, became the Philippine Islands.

I'm afraid geology provides the Philippines with a better-documented, though less exciting, origin. Their long and complicated and often bloody history, however, has known plenty of excitement. It includes invasions by Indonesians, Malays, the Chinese hordes of Kublai Khan, the Spaniards of Magellan, the Japanese of World War II, and twice of course by liberating American armies, climaxed by General Douglas MacArthur's famous "return."

Still, the special combination of islands (seven thousand of them) and remote valleys in high mountains has kept many moments of that fantastic history relatively unchanged by later or outside influences. The life on the islands, in fact, is the Philippines' best history book.

A few hours from Manila, one can move back centuries to odd periods of the Filipino past freakishly preserved here and there in the islands. If you travel north from the capital into the moun-

27

tains of Luzon, you enter a country and a culture that belong to one of the earliest chapters of Philippine history. From the summer capital of Baguio, a modern resort, you can swiftly reach the difficult country where the protohistoric tribes retreated before later invasions. You can hire a jeep to take you into the mountains, but far cheaper, only slightly less comfortable and infinitely more entertaining is the journey by one of the country buses.

Don't be put off by the warnings not to travel if the driver is drunk and to stop him if he goes too fast. Certainly the road is narrow and unnerving, but it winds through some of the most theatrically beautiful country I have ever seen, and the bus drivers, many of them mountain people themselves, know the road with comforting intimacy. You will probably, as a foreigner, be given the best seat—next to the driver. Behind you will be crowded the other passengers with their baskets of vegetables, their chickens and piglets. Everyone is very friendly, full of news, questions and gossip. You will hear the women singing soft lullabies to their babies, and the men giving a curious shrill whistle when they want the bus to stop.

As you go higher into the mountains, the jungle becomes a mixture of tropical tree ferns and bananas growing surrealistically between northern pines and oaks. You see great fields of calla lilies on the plateaus, and orchids and vines lace through the trees. The bus delivers mail at tiny villages clinging to the mountainside. If it is raining, the villagers you pass will be wearing rain capes woven of graded bamboo stems that flare and undulate with each movement—like some fantastic ballet.

Mountain women carrying wood or vegetables on their backs smile at the passengers and call out questions about the weather or prices in Baguio. Children peddle a Luzon delicacy called *balut* —a duck egg that is kept until the duckling inside is almost ready to be hatched. Then it is boiled and eaten warm—feathers, bones, everything except the shell. If a *balut* doesn't appeal, the people near you will offer to share their lunch of bananas and boiled sweet potatoes.

Far down the ravines are the emerald rice paddies; all around you is the dark green turmoil of forests and hills and beyond them the blue, blue mountains of the north. Sometime in the afternoon the bus dips into a cup-shaped valley where Bontoc, the capital of the mountain province, lies between a river and the surrounding hills. Suddenly the whole atmosphere has changed. You are in a small country town (three thousand people) in the heart of the country of the Igorots, the ancient settlers of Luzon, who until a few years ago were practicing head-hunters, and who still dress and farm and amuse themselves much as they did centuries ago.

In the Bontoc market place the Igorots from nearby villages bring their produce to exchange for rum, salt and a couple of hours of gambling. The men still wear the Igorot dress—something between a loincloth and a G-string, brightly colored and elaborately tasseled—and that is all. The flashy youths, before they are married, wear small baskets decorated with mirrors and buttons and scarlet thread on the backs of their heads; the older men have complicated tattoos, like Lord Fauntleroy collars, across shoulders and chest, marking them as successful head-hunters. The women also are tattooed, but only for decoration; on their hands and forearms are designs that give the effect of lacy opera gloves. They often wear only skirts made of a short piece of cloth woven in scarlet, blue or yellow stripes, with a sash that hangs down behind in a tasseled tail; some wear pieces of cloth over their shoulders and nearly all wind beads or snake vertebrae through their straight black hair.

In any of the villages around Bontoc, set among rice fields and fruit trees, you can see the simple but efficient organization of an Igorot town. A raised pavilion called the *ato* serves as a meeting place for the village elders; this is where they settle disputes and instruct the young men in the laws and customs of the village. The *ato* functions also as a magistrate's court, a place to arrange marriages, or perform religious ceremonies. In the old days a young man asked the permission of the *ato* before he went on a head-hunting expedition and sought advice on the best way to acquire an enemy's head.

In a long, low dormitory the young girls sleep until they marry. A similar dormitory houses the young men. When a marriage is contracted, money is collected to build the couple a home; water buffalo, called *carabao*, are fattened for the ceremony; pigs, chickens, eggs and rice are accumulated; and the entire village declares a fiesta lasting anywhere from two days to two entire weeks, with feasting, dancing, drinking and gambling every night.

If you are lucky enough to reach a village during such a fiesta, you simply join the wedding guests for huge meals of barbecued suckling pig with a sweetish garlic sauce, rice and chopped meat wrapped in banana leaves and baked, chickens and roast carabao, goat meat cooked in lime juice, and sometimes even stewed dog meat. The dancing will be subtle, complex and wonderfully exhilarating. By the firelight in the plaza, young men beat out rhythms on metal gongs and move, half hunched over, in a circle in one of the traditional dances of jubilation, while outside the circle, girls with outstretched arms and nervous feet pursue the patterns of their own dance.

If no fiesta is scheduled, you can still see something of Bontoc dancing for the price of a *ganta* (about four pounds) of salt; you may even get to see fragments of the old head-hunting dance. It is bad luck to perform the full original dance without a genuine head; on the rare occasions when the Igorots have used a wooden head as a substitute they claim that they have been visited by misfortune. However, even a watered-down version is remarkably chilling, with its rigid, almost hypnotic steps and stamping, deafening gongs, and the wild climax of the spear-and-shield dance, as two young men leap about in the firelight before the scarcely-moving chorus, the shadowed figures of the musicians and the silent watchers.

Northeast of Bontoc, along another precipitous mountain road through dense rain forests, is Ifugao country, another of the earliest Philippine settlements. In Banaue, the tiny Ifugao capital—just a muddy mountain lane with a scattering of houses and shops—the dress, dancing, language and customs are again peculiarly their own, the product of centuries of isolated life. All around Banaue are the rice terraces constructed more than two thousand years ago, and climbing in great glassy steps four thousand feet up the mountainsides.

There among the rice fields, ingeniously banked and irrigated, the Ifugaos farm their land, produce their delicious rice wine called *baya*, live in houses built on stilts and with heavy thatches of palm leaves. Many of the houses are built of a fine reddish wood which gives you the odd but pleasant sensation of living inside a cigar box. In them Ifugao women weave the heavy cotton for their skirts on ancient looms while men hammer out silver and gold jewelry. In rainy weather the men carve the crude figures which have become famous in the Philippines for their wonderful humor and eerie sense of the grotesque—strange devils, animals and humans—including a small wooden man with incredible distress on his face; he has suddenly found himself pregnant.

31

If the northern mountains of Luzon have protected the oldest living culture in the Philippines, almost all the other islands have sheltered comparable, but fainter, traces of races and civilizations that have flourished there—the Negritos of Zambales, the pygmies of Mindoro, the tree dwellers of the rain forests in the central islands. Of all such pockets of leftover history, probably the most dramatic and distinctive are the Moslem settlements of the fourteenth century. Their ports and villages are mostly on the big southern island of Mindanao and spread south through all the tiny, magical islands to the equator.

The Spaniards, when they reached these islands, called the people *Moros* and the name, to the distress of many of the peaceful settlements, has stuck. For, to the Spaniards, the Moros were at the best "fierce" and at the worst "treacherous." Every generation or so Spain began a campaign to bring the Moslems under Spanish rule and each time Spain was defeated. The Americans, when they took over the Philippines, had little more success. At least one company of American cavalry was hacked to death with spears and krises in the hills behind Jolo, the capital of the Sulu group of islands, before the Americans, deciding on a calmer course of expediency, gave the Moslems special privileges and a high measure of autonomy and won a precarious peace. Even today the Moslems of the south are far from subdued. The Philippine central government declares the islands a "special area" and a curious dual government exists, with the provincial officials appointed from Manila functioning alongside of Moslem *dattus* or village chiefs, and *agama* courts which administer Moslem law.

In spite of all this, the Sulu Sea is possibly the only really romantic place left in the world. From Borneo curving northward to the southern Philippines a ribbon of thousands of tiny islands provides almost every storybook notion of adventure and enchantment. From the days, a thousand years ago, when the Sulus were the headquarters and fiercely guarded hide-out of the notorious Malay pirates who plundered the Philippine coasts and terrorized the shipping of all the southern seas, piracy has been a lucrative and thriving tradition. The fabulous stories of wealth and beauty drew adventurers to the islands from all over Asia, but the Malay pirates never lost their dominion of the seas even when the Moslems took the land. The islands are still full of stories of hidden treasure, frightful raids of revenge, and mighty battles at sea. If you walk down to the wharf in Jolo, the main port on the largest island of the Sulus, any Joloano will point out to you the narrow Moro *vintas* which defy capture, and he may add casually, "I see the smugglers are in from Borneo." The next day, instead of the silks and ivory, slaves and gold which were the loot of the ancient pirates, the Jolo markets will be filled with English whisky and gin from British possessions in Asia, or American cigarettes or French perfumes or pearls or sarongs from Indonesia.

Island cultures have an almost classic appeal to travelers, and scattered through the Sulu Sea are some of the strangest and most fascinating islands of the world. An endlessly glamorous way to spend a week or ten days is to hire a small boat in Jolo and sail among the rocks and reefs and beaches of the Sulus. The water is very deep, the currents are rapid and tricky, but the climate is magnificent, with warm days and cool nights and steady winds. In the equatorial sunsets, flaming across the sky in great banners of green and gold, you will see Moro boats, slim and fast, carrying big square sails in elegant stripes of yellow, gray and black. Each has a double outrigger to give it stability enough to sail to China through heavy seas.

In the Sulu Sea are the great pearl banks, so famous that even six hundred years ago a Chinese adventurer reported that Sulu pearls were "whiter and rounder than those of India. Their price is very high"—a reputation that continues to this day. Another tremendous source of revenue for the Sulus comes from the five Turtle Islands, which look in every way like the conventional picture of a tropical paradise—palm trees, sandy beaches, clear sea water and coral rocks, except that once every eighteen days thousands of turtles totter up the shore to lay their eggs (between 100 and 145 each) in the sand and scuttle back to the water, leaving hundreds of thousands of eggs to be exported among the islands, where they are a most popular delicacy.

Almost every island has its special distinction. A tiny Sulu island called Siasi declared war on the United States all by itself. Another island, Laminasa, is only two hundred yards wide and a kilometer long, but twelve thousand people live on it, weaving the finest nipa mats in the Philippines and selling them from Luzon to Jolo for floor and wall coverings. Sibutu has the finest dancing in the country and a curious technique of intricate etching on cane. Kabingaan is an island only at low tide: a few hours later it vanishes under several feet of water, but ten thousand people live there on houseboats moored permanently to the sand bank. They live by taking their small boats to the rich Sulu fishing grounds, where they catch hundreds of varieties of fish I had never seen before—clear tropical colors, striped or spotted, with fins like filmy wings or with beards or with teeth like fangs. By exchanging part of their catch for supplies and rice, a Kabingaano may spend his entire life on boats and never set foot on dry land.

You also can get a flavor of both the old days of lawlessness as well as the modern, more peaceful, but still exotic life, in the port of Jolo. In the harbor are boats from all the islands, and around the small Chinese shops and stalls on the water front you will see bare-chested Malay sailors, women in batik sarongs, traders from other Sulu ports carrying daggers in their belts, women from remote islands with rare parrots.

Beyond the harbor of Jolo is the cove where the sea gypsies live, ocean-going nomads who move from island to island, trading a little, fishing a little, even smuggling a little, staying in Jolo a couple of days or a couple of months. They live with their families on boats so narrow that two people cannot sit side by side in them. For protection from rain they have a flimsy arrangement of palm leaves spread over a bamboo frame. Strips of octopus are stretched across the outriggers to dry. A deeply sunburned woman squats in the stern beside an earthenware pot filled with live charcoal, mixing shredded coconut meat with cassava, or neatly wrapping this staple in banana leaves for a meal to be eaten out at sea. The children drag the nets up the beach to dry, or suddenly dive off the boat with their homemade spears to get the small, delicious scarlet fish that frequent the shallow water.

Near the cove of the sea gypsies live the Samals, amphibious people who dwell in wooden houses built on stilts over the water and connected with rickety paths of planks and bamboos. While the men fish the women stay home, decorate themselves with tiny pearls, paint their faces with a dead-white make-up of rice powder and spices, and weave thin, checked cotton sarongs.

Anywhere in Jolo you will see the Moro men and women in trousers of intense green, purple, pink and flame, stylishly cut about three inches above the ankle. Across their shoulders, and sometimes over their heads, the Moro women wrap contrasting loops of cloth, while the men wear tight buttoned jackets. After the wharf, the most interesting place in Jolo is the market, a huge, smelly clutter of stalls and eating places where you will be unable to name any of the dozens of varieties of fish that are offered for sale. Here you can see and taste Jolo's incredible profusion of fruit including the famous durian (whose skin smells so horrid that most foreigners never taste it, though if you eat the flesh you probably will prefer it to any other tropical fruit). Here you can buy local spices, betel nut, reed mats, wood carvings, steel daggers, and Japanese umbrellas.

In Parang, a village about half an hour from Jolo, there is another, smaller pearling industry. For a few cents a couple of the sea gypsies will row you out to the pearling canoes. The shallow water is so clear a green that you can easily see the sea urchins and anemones among the coral rocks and sand of the ocean bottom. In the deeper water the pearl divers, in tight little breechcloths, with no equipment except homemade glasses to protect their eyes, topple off their slender canoes and are often lost in the dark green water for three minutes at a time. Long after you are certain that they cannot possibly hold their breath another second, they break the surface, wet black hair slicked against their heads, a smile of success or a look of resignation on their faces.

When a diver comes up with a huge gray disc of an oyster, he will bring it to your boat and open it, prying it apart with a quick twist of a sliver of bamboo. He scrapes out the oyster and kneads it with his fingers, because the best and roundest pearls are found in the oyster flesh. He will probably give you the oyster meat. He saves the mother shell, however, for out of this pearl buttons and ornaments will be made.

None of the divers found a pearl while I was watching. In twenty years of diving they expect to get about a hundred pearls. They work the local oyster beds, the great pearl banks of the eastern Sulu Sea, and as far south as the Celebes. After one such expedition I was served, in Parang, one of the strangest meals of my life, composed of the favorite dishes of the village—Jolo rice (which is supposed to have a special perfume), shark meat, dried sting ray, oyster stew, the liver of a fish called pogot dressed with lime juice and chilis, and a plate of what looked like dented ping-pong balls and turned out to be turtle eggs.

After you eat in any of the villages around Jolo, you can call in professional musicians and dancers who will play bamboo xylophones and fiddles and sing the songs of their Moro ancestors. Or they will perform the newest and most popular dance, *da-ling, da-ling,* in which the dancers clatter their sandals on the floor and flirt discreetly as they sing intimate descriptions of the joys of beauty and the pleasures of love.

In the early evening you hear the musicians shuffle away down the village road, still singing softly to each other, turning back occasionally to wave at you or to glance up at the inland hills where the fierce guerrillas still claim their ancient autocratic rule of the islands.

While the Sulu Sea maintains its own turbulent and romantic life almost entirely separate from the rest of the Philippines, the more peaceful settlements of Moslems are on the island of Mindanao, next to Luzon, the largest island of the Philippines. It is filled with the evocative names that belong in the distant adventures of sixteenth-century sailors and explorers —Cagayan de Oro, Misamis, beautiful Pagil Bay with the dark blue sails of its boats, its gray waters flanked by mountains. Most celebrated of all, perhaps, is Zamboanga, on the westernmost peninsula of Mindanao, a city so appealing that in the old days a girl used to sing to her sweetheart, "Don't you go, don't you go to far Zamboanga" because the women there are so fair that if they smile at a man he is lost.

Even today, beaten and changed by the war, the Japanese occupation and the American return, Zamboanga hasn't lost its
charm. The women are still fair, the beaches with their many-
colored sands are still splendid, the Moslem traders still stand
beside their flamboyant boats, bargaining over spices, and at
night the harbor is still lit with flares from their departing ships.

But of all the towns in Mindanao the one I like the best is
Dansalan. Outside all the first-floor windows of a Filipino home
are banks of flowers in pots and window boxes. Purple tree
orchids and white butterfly orchids hang from the eaves. The
windows made of small sea shells, pared down until they are
translucent, are opened to reveal more flowers inside the house
and banks of blooms between the rooms. But around Dansalan
is the most lavish flowering I saw in the islands.

Gardens are jammed with cannas, lilies and bougainvillaea and
separated from each other with hedges of hibiscus. Narrow canals
which circle the houses are entirely obscured by mauve lilies
and water hyacinths. The women dress their hair in a great
loop on one side of the head and decorate it with the flame-colored
flower from an African tulip tree. Men tie their sarongs in a
dashing flounce at the waist and emphasize it with an oleander,
or they tuck a frangipani blossom into their headcloth.

Dansalan is famous in the Philippines for many things—
its Moslem culture, its scenery, its invigorating climate, its
pagoda-shaped mosques and inlaid metal work, but most of
all for its beautiful music. Small gongs called *kulingtan* are
played by the prettiest girls in the neighborhood, and the accompanying drums and the big gongs are played by young men
who, traditionally, are in love with the girl musicians. Fast and

tricky rhythms express the changes of musical mood, of fighting, love and religious dedication.

The singers perform with no accompaniment but a gentle beating on a spittoon placed at their knees. The first singer, formally dressed in a bright sarong, crouches on one knee, an open fan in his hand, and announces his song with a curious persuasive humming, like a dove. This, I was told, is "just to make graciousness." The words when they begin are always improvised and usually start with compliments to the audience or to any individual who catches the singer's eye.

In reply, the second singer answers the compliments in even more florid terms, and then suddenly sings a story, perhaps about a girl locked in a tower while her lover wanders desolate outside. As the story progresses the singer begins to dance. He picks up an extra fan and flutters the two together like a butterfly to represent the grace of the heroine. Almost every song concludes with a fight in which the hero is victorious. The singer crouches on the floor, he dances, he leaps, he uses his folded fan as a sword, and finally he wins the battle. The spectators are weak from cheering and everybody feels pleased to live in Dansalan.

For the most part it is in the far-away islands, in the forbidding mountains and among the groups with independent cultures and traditions that the truest remnants of pre-Spanish history remain. In the lowlands the Spaniards first established their garrisons and towns and missions, using those centers to expand their rule. Because Manila was one of the earliest and largest settlements, accepted even in the sixteenth century as the capital of the Philippines, the strongest Spanish influence grew there.

But in the last sixty years the influences in the city have been mixed. Today the life most reminiscent of the old Spanish days remains (with a brooding sense of transience) only in the Visayan Islands—Cebu, Negros, Panay—across the center of the Philippines.

A friend of mine described a formal ball given in Iloilo by one of the old, distinguished families. It opened in the traditional way with ladies in fabulous *ternos* and their escorts dancing a quadrille called the *rigodon d'honneur*. Afterward everyone danced the Lanceros—a formal Spanish dance popular among the aristocracy of the last century. "But," my friend continued, "there were too few servants to keep the place in perfect order. The parquet hadn't been polished, the furniture showed signs of wear. It was a brave effort—but an *effort*."

However, the conversation was all in Spanish. The food and wine were Spanish and the temperament recalled the leisurely, spacious past—long afternoon siestas, formal evenings with the daughter of the house singing a *kundiman*, a sad, sweet ballad about love, and accompanying herself on the guitar.

Not that all plantation life is entirely like that. Victorias on the island of Negros is one of the Philippines' most progressive and largest plantations, with the only sugar refinery in the country. Good housing, schools and excellent hospitals are provided for the employees, but, most revolutionary of all, in the heart of the old colonial atmosphere, is Victorias' modern church, with paintings by the *avant garde* artist Alfonso Ossorio and wooden images of the Holy Family made by local craftsmen—a Virgin and child, both Filipino in feature and dress instead of the usual blue-eyed blonds, and a Filipino Christ on the cross.

In other parts of the Visayas many of the plantation owners

are closing up the old country houses for the gaudier attractions of the city. Inevitably they add to the government's most persistent headache—land reform.

Of all the many influences that have reached the Philippines, the most recent and in many ways the most effective has been the American. Like the Spanish rulers, the Americans made Manila their headquarters and it is in the capital that one sees the most obvious signs of American influence; from Manila American ways of thinking and living, American gadgets or policies spread unevenly to the rest of the country. This newest layer of history has added another dimension to a city that already is a composite of a dozen civilizations.

This tumultuous mixture of races and cultures and personalities is perhaps the first aspect of Manila that impresses the visitor. The wide green boulevard that follows the beautiful curve of Manila Bay (one of the world's largest and best harbors) is named for Admiral Dewey. As you move away from the clean American lines of the sea front, you will find streets and squares with Spanish names crisscrossed with, say, Nebraska or Tennessee Street, or with the brave names of the Philippines' own heroes, Rizal, Quezon, Mabini.

In Manila you can lead an entirely Spanish life, if you desire, among the large community of Spanish businessmen, officials, visitors and journalists. You can eat your meals in the correct atmosphere of the Spanish Club or drink Spanish wine in the informal charm of El Bodegon as you listen to Spanish songs and guitar music, or you can go to Spanish parties in Spanish homes. Only Manila's high cost of living and the faces in the street as you drive home in the early morning will remind you that you are half a world away from Madrid. Equally, you can live an

American life with all the necessary surroundings of American clubs, restaurants, soda fountains, movies, plays and people. Or a Chinese life. Or even, in a small way, an Indian life.

The Filipinos themselves move easily among the cultures—adapting, borrowing, using in their own lives whatever is pleasant or appropriate or convenient or stylish from other countries and other people. A Filipino woman may wear an American dress for lunch, or appear in a *patadiong* with its characteristic starched gauze sleeves—itself an adaptation of the nineteenth-century Spanish dress—and wrap a short skirt, a remnant of her own Tagalog ancestry, over the long foreign skirt. If she is fairly well off, she may live in a house that would certainly do credit to any town in, say, Southern California. She will eat food that owes something to the cuisines of China, India, Spain, America and her own special province of the Philippines. Her husband may drive to his American-style office in an American car, but quite possibly he will wear the loose, thin, beautifully embroidered Philippine shirt called a *barong Tagalog* which is far more suitable to the Manila climate. They will probably speak Tagalog to their servants, Spanish to their parents and English to each other. Often a remark will begin in English and end with a Spanish phrase or a small Tagalog joke. A Spanish friend once gave me an example of this. He was traveling in a train and sitting across from him were a Filipino family. At one point the woman said casually to her husband, "Cierra la window por que nos vamos catchear un cold." ("Close the window, else we are going to catch cold.")

Into all this free adoption of foreign cultures and ways of life and thought, however, the Filipinos always seem to inject certain characteristics that are peculiarly their own. If they have adopted the Spanish religion it is without a Spanish sense of tragedy. If they have taken over American aspects of living, it doesn't leave, on them, the lines of anxiety around their mouths, the nervousness about success, the unremitting drive. Everywhere the Filipinos display the qualities for which they are best loved —an overwhelming sense of generosity and hospitality, a sort of gentle gaiety that can be mistaken, by foreigners, for softness, a great courtesy, a sensitivity that can degenerate to touchiness and hurt feelings at the lightest affront but which is also responsible for the flawless manners of a Filipino, for his great warmth and consideration for the stranger.

But the amalgamation of foreign influences in Manila has its puzzling aspects, and the emergence of the character and life that is truly Filipino is a matter that has concerned and troubled Manila's growing group of talented writers and poets. To their more intimate eyes Manila presents disturbing contradictions and strange compounds. As one of the best and most versatile among them, Nick Joaquin, describes it, the "special temper of the city and its people," is a "combination of primitive mysticism and slick modernity . . . pert girls dancing with abandon all night long in the cabarets and fleeing in black veils to hear the first Mass at dawn; boys in the latest, loudest Hollywood styles, with American slang in their mouths and the crucifix on their breasts; streets ornate with movie palaces and jammed with traffic through which leaf-crowned and barefooted penitents carried a Black Christ in procession . . . the crowds and hot dust and skeleton ruins and gay cabarets."

Another Filipino once remarked: "We have lived for four hundred years in a convent and for fifty years in Hollywood. When are we going to come to grips with real life?" And, indeed, the foreigner in Manila is plagued by an uneasy sense of unreality too. It is difficult to search under the shiny surface of

Manila for the life that one thinks of, dimly, as genuinely Filipino.

Probably the most attractive attribute of the Filipinos is that they, more than any other nation in Asia, have an ability to laugh at themselves, a saving sense of the absurd. However, many of their most distinguished writers see tragedy in their long domination (cruel or kindly) by the foreigner. Zulueta da Costa, acknowledged as the nation's leading poet, writes: "We, the Filipinos of today, are soft, easy-going, parasitic, frivolous, inconstant, indolent, inefficient."

Rather bitterly, he adds, "We are secure under the Stars and Stripes." To the readers of his best-known poem, *Like the Molave*, to Filipinos who speak three foreign languages fluently but can only "lisp a little Tagalog," to his countryman who "dreams to the grand tune of the American dream," he suggests a revaluation of the true Filipino culture, he begs for a return to a different national dignity, a new maturity that will bring with it an acceptance of the Filipino as a Filipino, not as the Little Brown Brother of a Western nation.

It is a theme that is often repeated in the writing and conversation of Philippine intellectuals, and eventually the visitor begins to wonder whether "the Great American Dream" is not perhaps obscuring the urgency of "the heat and the dust and the rats . . . the patched-up tenements where four or five families lived huddled together in each room and did their cooking and washing in the foul passages." Even the stranger is compelled to look beyond the wonderfully attractive glitter of westernized Manila life, the magnificent parties, the fine hotels and restaurants, the modern apartment houses, the beauty of old Spanish cathedrals, to the swampy outskirts of the city or even the bombed-out lots in Intramuros where thousands of squatters jam into any available space, making what shelter they can out of crumbling buildings, and living with their children in a mess of pigs, filth, disease and poverty. In fact, under the lacquer of western Manila life there are the problems and conditions that belong to all Asian countries.

If these aspects of the nature and effect of American influence are disturbingly expressed by a minority, one comfort, at least, to the American traveler is that Filipinos as a whole seem to be quite genuinely fond of Americans as individuals; and that as a nation they are the closest friends America has. Manila as a city and the Philippines in general are probably the most flattering and pleasing places in the world for an American to visit today.

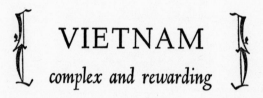

VIETNAM
complex and rewarding

THE PHILIPPINES ARE PERHAPS THE EASIEST place in Southeast Asia for a Westerner to start a tour of the region. There is virtually no language barrier, living conditions are comfortable—in some cases luxurious—many hotels, restaurants, clubs, movies, shops, even private houses are air-conditioned against Manila's debilitating heat, the food and ways of life are not too alarmingly foreign, the people are receptive, friendly and hospitable.

From this warmly welcoming atmosphere we went (again because geographical accident made it the most convenient place to go next) to the most difficult Southeast Asian country for a foreigner, Vietnam. After five years of Japanese occupation and nearly ten years of anti-French warfare, the country was, naturally enough, exhausted, low both in human and natural resources, intent on its internal problems without much time for foreigners and tourists. Streams of refugees were coming in from the Communist North Vietnam; many thousands of them jammed the capital, Saigon, and the countryside around it. The city was crowded still further by the teams of United Nations observers and their staffs, with the personnel of relief agencies working to ease the shortage of food, clothing, medical supplies and the inevitable economic dislocations. Periodically the city would be flooded with thousands of French soldiers waiting for troop ships and transport planes to take them back to France—

all part of the enormous, complicated French evacuation program. As the French administration shrank, the American embassy and its related agencies grew with overwhelming speed. It quickly became clear that the vacuum of foreign influence left by the retreating French was to be filled by the Americans—a tricky and thankless job—and this in turn made for considerable friction even among the foreigners in Vietnam.

The last time I had been in Vietnam, about five years earlier, I had arrived by ship from Hong Kong, moving slowly up the Saigon River for several hours from the coast, staring at the wide, flat marshlands through which the river curved in great loops, a shiny ribbon the color of mud. We docked at the end of the Rue Catinat, the main street of the city that runs straight through the heart of the shopping and business district from the river to the cathedral. We gazed at the stucco hotels, office buildings, apartment houses along the water front, mostly painted a yellowish-white (which we later learned was locally known as "Saigon cream"). Below us was the Quai des Fleurs, further along there were pushcarts and small wooden stalls with fruit and vegetables. Across the street were sidewalk cafés, and on the walls beside them were French advertisements for French drinks and medicines. Except for the faces of the Vietnamese on the streets and their clothes—the hats shaped like limpet shells, the flapping trousers and tunics—Saigon could have been a French provincial town at a calm moment of a very hot summer.

This time we arrived in Saigon by plane and I couldn't help contrasting this first view of the city with my last impression of it. Here the crowded, tense confusion was immediately apparent. The newly expanded airport, built to cope with the increased military demands as the war intensified, was already shabby and inadequate for the vast strains of recent months. Exasperated and overworked airport officials told us in a variety of languages and gestures that they were hopelessly understaffed, and in any case what could they possibly do with planes arriving or leaving at forty-five-second intervals during the peak hours?

Somehow, by bus, or by a lift from some helpful stranger with a car or jeep, passengers managed to get into Saigon to find all hotels, boardinghouses—French, Chinese, Vietnamese—even American billets packed to capacity and beyond. Driving through the city, the battered, rundown surface of Saigon could be seen at once. Of course, even on our previous visit, that initial, untroubled vision of the city soon turned out to be quite remote from the truth, but the thing that impressed me this time was that the exigencies of peace seemed to impose an even greater stress on the city. There were all the aftermath of war and all the demands of rehabilitation to cope with.

From my hotel window I could see the river, and instead of the small trading ships, the country craft, the Chinese junks, there were the gray-painted ships of the American navy that were helping to bring refugees down from Hanoi. Periodically, long shuffling lines of them would appear on the quay; many were carrying babies; some had only a salvaged cooking pot or a small bundle of clothes. Temporary kitchens were set up to give them a meal before they were crowded into trucks and buses and sent off to the villages of tents set up outside the city, or to the deserted French army barracks.

Even during the time that we were in Vietnam, conditions improved, but I doubt if Saigon will ever again be the city that the French used to call "The Paris of the Orient." It was still studded with reminders of that old, lost, glittering colonial life, but now with all the marks of decay. The Opera House, bravely built at the intersection of the Rue Catinat with one of the main cross boulevards, had its lavish interior shattered by hand grenades thrown by revolutionaries in the city during the fighting. At one time the ladies of the colony used to turn out in all their finery to see the touring theatrical companies from France that performed there. It had been converted to temporary, crowded, unsanitary quarters for refugees. Fewer and fewer of the chic dress shops along the Rue Catinat and its side arcades show French styles and accessories. The old palace of the French governor has been renamed Norodom and is now occupied by the Vietnamese president.

Eventually, of course, conditions in Saigon will settle down, and then perhaps the city will become genuinely Vietnamese. Already there are signs of this—new Vietnamese restaurants have started and are doing good business from both Vietnamese and foreign clients. The Vietnamese theater is growing and developing, occupying some auditoriums that used to show French movies, building others of their own. You now see Vietnamese in some of the clubs, swimming pools, hotels that used to be reserved (either by regulations or by tacit agreement) for foreigners only.

The Chinese life of Saigon—in the huge Chinese "suburb" called Cholon—is asserting itself with a new authority, for the Chinese have in the past and certainly will in the future affect the life and livelihood of the Vietnamese much more than their ex-rulers, the French. Vietnamese and foreigners alike are deserting the French *boîtes* or night clubs of Saigon (even when they feature a *trépidante et très sexy* singer) for the big brassy dance halls of Cholon with their Vietnamese and Chinese taxi dancers, their brilliant lighting and enormous orchestras. There they like to dance the *lamtong*, the fabulously popular dance

that has swept Southeast Asia, to music that is somewhere between Western swing and Chinese film music. The dance itself
is a curious adaptation of ballroom dancing (without its intimacy) and individual Asian dance traditions (without their
intricacy).

People also seem to prefer the Chinese chophouses to the small,
expensive French restaurants, and even though some of the
better-known restaurants of Cholon still echo Paris in their
names—*Tour d'Ivoire* or *Palais de Jade*—you eat Chinese food
or adaptations of it there accompanied by the incessant clatter
of mahjong chips from the neighboring rooms. With all these
indications of a changing way of life in Vietnam, Saigon remains
a strange international hodgepodge, a city in transition with
fascinating remnants—some sad, some hopeful—of its short,
extraordinary history.

For the first time in seventeen years you can travel in Vietnam
beyond Saigon, and it is both a saddening and an exciting experience to visit this country, torn in two. In many towns in this
long, curving country that follows the bulge of the Indo-Chinese
coast, you can still see scars from the long, grinding fight that has
been the chief tragedy of Vietnam's recent history. But since
South Vietnam became a republic in the fall of 1955, the lovely
tropical countryside, the villages, the forests and the seaside are
all accessible again, and with them there's the distinctive appeal
of a complex, often rewarding life.

For anyone interested in the future of Asia, here, in miniature,
are most of the problems that characterize this huge, neglected
continent today—from the urgent necessity for internal reforms
to the conflict with Communist ideology and the gradual
building of democratic procedures in a country that has known

neither independence nor democracy for a hundred years. But Vietnam is not simply a concentrated lesson in political science —there are many pleasant places to visit and some remote parts of the country that are both strange and beautiful.

For many of your pleasures in Vietnam you must still thank the French. As soon as you arrive in Saigon you are aware even now of the lingering influence of French civilization. In the center of the city, around the shops and hotels, it is the Vietnamese women in their national clothes who sometimes look incongruous, for French manners, styles and habits continue to lie like lacquer over everything. When the French came here, in the middle of the last century, Saigon, which had never been much of a town, became an important port and took on new dignity. It acquired an ornate opera house, a red brick cathedral, charming homes, boulevards, sidewalk cafés and the ubiquitous advertisements for *Byrrh* or *Bastos* cigarettes.

Even now Saigon offers a fair facsimile of French life, complete with delicious French food and wine, Jean Gabin movies, a *Cercle Sportif* and those frightful *apéritifs* that taste like cough medicine. But the new spirit of republicanism has shown itself in a variety of ways. The de-luxe French specialty shops, with their perfumes and gloves and neckties from the Rue de la Paix, have closed up, and their owners have gone back to France or perhaps to North Africa. The wonderful French cheeses, the pâtés and other canned goods from the *metropole* that used to gladden the foreigner here are scarce and expensive. All streets bear Vietnamese names; the High Commissioner's palace is now the "Palace of Independence" and, in keeping with its changed status, the Lycée Chasseloup-Laubat, named after a famous colonialist, is now the Lycée Jean-Jacques Rousseau. The National Assembly meets in the refurbished Opera House, and the French military camps have been taken over by the American-equipped Vietnamese army. French cultural influence, however, is still strong, and a special mission, headed by the former chief of the French information services here, is successfully working to keep alive French education in Vietnam.

The French built Vietnam's first holiday resorts. From an isolated, barren point of land, they made Cap Saint-Jacques a beach town of wide boulevards, shady pastel villas and French hotels where you can eat the tiny, excellent shrimps and oysters of the China Sea, and dance in the tepid tropical evenings under the coconut palms by the phosphorescent ocean surf. But there is little in Cap Saint-Jacques with its yellow sandy coves, rock-encrusted promontories and scrubby tamarisks to remind you of Vietnam. It differs widely from the flat, typical delta country of South Vietnam you see on the two-hour drive back to Saigon. First, there's a dark tangle of mangrove swamps, then miles and miles of moist, green rice country broken occasionally by a village of palm-leaf houses, a fragment of forest for some reason never cleared or the symmetrical avenues of rubber trees.

Probably the pleasantest resort built by the French is Dalat, five thousand feet up in the mountains north of Saigon. It is a relatively new town that became popular because it was close enough to offer the homesick colonial a cool weekend away from the steamy climate of the capital. Special gardens grow "European" vegetables—lettuce, asparagus, cucumbers—and it is one of the few towns where fresh milk is available. In the dry season there are great fields of roses and pinks, forest clearings filled with violets and, here and there, clear yellow clouds of mimosa. Almost any walk leads to a magnificent view of the chilly, purple mountains. But best of all, from the viewpoint of the Westerner, warm clothes and a fire are necessary in the evenings.

Recently Dalat has been recognized for two other distinctions —its excellent hunting (as varied as the more publicized game of Africa and India, and far cheaper), and its extraordinary mountain tribes. In a way the two are connected, because the hill people are noted for their uncanny hunting skill. Throughout the mountains and forests to which they retreated during ancient, forgotten invasions, the hill people became expert hunters for protection and for food. Surrounded by elephant, tiger, deer, boar, roebuck, black bear, buffalo and any number of game birds, they learned to track and kill even the elephants with crossbows, padding barefoot and half naked through the jungle.

Although their strange little villages, their huts covered with a thatch that reaches almost to the ground, seem temporary and casual, and though they often travel great distances on foot through their dangerous country, they are not nomads. They cultivate mountain rice and cotton, keep animals (some for sacrifice and some for food and labor), hunt, weave and maintain a highly organized society. The women wrap themselves in hand-woven black, blue and red cottons and decorate themselves with ivory and bead necklaces and with great hoops of ivory thrust through their pierced ears. The dashing young men wear a brief loincloth, and many still tie their long hair in a high, loose knot through which they stick a couple of arrows.

In the old days the annual exodus of the hill people to the coast was a very special event. In the dry season after the harvest, the tribes marched down to the sea towns to pay their taxes and make a few purchases. According to the old men who remember the hill life before the war, it was an exciting occasion. For days the women prepared food and rice wine and selected their finest embroidered cloth for barter; the men collected animal hides and ivory, pinewood and surplus rice. A girl would coyly tell her young man that unless he bought her a fancy city skirt on the coast he would forever call her "sister."

Eventually, whole families would set off with children, food and animals on a journey that lasted several weeks. They stopped at hill villages along the way for feasting and dancing and added new members to their festive procession. When they finally reached the coast they exchanged their hill products for store clothes and the gay city life, and then returned to their mountains for the rest of the year.

Those old journeys remain only in the nostalgic conversation of the elders, but even now the shorter travels of the hill people are accompanied by music and celebrations, and in the evenings, either in forest camp or village, they tell stories of their journeyings and recite their old legends. Usually these legends are full of spirits and the transmigration of souls into animals and plants, and they give a curious and vivid supernatural life to the jungle. A famous legend, for instance, concerns two mountain girls, Gliu and Glah, who were goatherds. One day a prince dispatched a raven with a pair of shoes in its beak to find a girl who could wear the shoes. Gliu was the only one the shoes fit and she married the prince. The jealous Glah killed Gliu one day when the prince was away, and buried her, hoping to replace her in the prince's affections. But Gliu's spirit entered a clump of bamboos and revealed herself to the prince. Glah cut down the bamboos and Gliu's spirit entered a bird and dropped a betel box at the prince's feet to identify herself. Glah killed the bird, but its spirit moved to a papaya tree. After endless similar complications, the spirit finally returned to Gliu's body, which came to life again.

Many of their stories concern bravery. Probably the most highly prized quality among them is a kind of careful courage which makes them wonderful guides. If hill people accompany you on an expedition into the mountain jungles, whether you do it in full style on elephants or more simply on foot, you are certain of good hunting—and entertainment.

A pleasant, slow and strangely old-fashioned kind of life still continues on the big French rubber plantations. Most of the estates are set in the famous Red Earth districts of South Vietnam near the Cambodian border where rubber grows best. Traditionally the planters are glad of an opportunity to meet travelers, and it is fairly easy to arrange a visit to a rubber plantation and to taste for a few days the sort of Somerset Maugham atmosphere now rapidly disappearing in other parts of Asia.

The plantation houses are big and cool, with deeply shaded verandahs and polished red tile floors. From almost any window, you can see the tidy forest of rubber trees, set in endless, regular rows and holding between them a perpetual green gloom. After a few years, the planters say, any other landscape seems cluttered and direct sunlight becomes too harsh for charm. Plantation life moves according to its own special rules and timing, beginning before dawn with the distant bells and chatter of the Vietnamese plantation workers, continuing through the long afternoon siestas in shuttered rooms with the looped-up mosquito curtain making a shadowy canopy overhead and the occasional quick wriggle of a lizard on the wall, into the evenings and a casual drive of perhaps fifty miles to call on a neighbor.

On festivals and other special occasions the plantation workers hold dances on an earthen floor decorated with bamboo stems and roofed with a lattice of palm leaves and flowers. Nearly always they do the *lamtong*, in which the girl, as often as not, does the inviting, dancing before her choice until he joins her. Then she quickly turns away and leads her partner through as complicated a series of dance patterns as she can concoct. A *lamtong* may last all night, ending only when the plantation workers must return to the rubber trees to replace the bowls that catch the sticky white latex flowing like thick cream from shallow spiral gashes in the trees.

Although so much of Vietnamese life is strongly French in influence, gradually a new character is emerging that is culturally and historically compounded of Vietnam's own past, while the French legacies gradually shrink in importance.

Perhaps the single most significant factor of Vietnam's history is that here Asia's two biggest cultural influences met—the Chinese, expanding southward, and the Indian pushing east through Southeast Asia. The nation is dotted with evidences of both, and of the fusion of the two. In all Vietnam's beautiful coastal towns there are reminders of the country's complicated past. Ha-tien, for example, on the Gulf of Siam, is an ancient Khmer town, built when the Hindu cultural domination was at its height; yet in the bay the boats are Chinese, wooden junks with bat-wing sails and prows decorated with the Chinese protective symbol, the "lucky eye." In one of the junks, sheltered from the grilling sun by a braided bamboo awning, you can sail out to the islands in the Gulf where tortoises are captured for their shells and where fragments of old Hindu forts and monuments still remain.

In those distant days Vietnam's history was monotonously full of wars. Like all the rest of the Indo-Chinese peninsula it had fought and been fought over even before recorded history. The first invaders entered the country from the north, pushing the original inhabitants into the long mountain range that runs down the country like a gigantic spine. Gradually, through wars, conquests and political maneuverings the wide coastal strip of

Indo-China—from China in the north to the Gulf of Siam in the south—was separated into three states, Cochin China, Annam and Tonkin. Each produced its own rulers, armies, civilizations and special prides. Each attempted with varying success to maintain its independence. Cochin China, with its capital in Saigon, was for hundreds of years a vassal of Cambodia where the Khmer kings ruled in unimaginable magnificence from the ninth to the thirteenth century. As the Khmer empire disintegrated, the people of Annam began to infiltrate south to what they called The Land of the Deer. At first they merely traded with the hill tribes, but later came their armies to seize Cochin China.

Meanwhile Annam itself had its troubles. It had been ruled, more than a thousand years ago, by the Cham kings, who had also been subdued by the Khmer rulers and had been forced to guard their frontiers against their northern neighbors of Tonkin. And to complete the pattern, Tonkin had been annexed by China, and even in times of relative peace had paid a nervous tribute to the distant emperors of Peking.

On the coast of the China Sea, two of the past glories of Annam still remain—Nhatrang, with its beautiful harbor and beaches where the tide is like the "roar of a tiger" and where glass-bottomed boats take you out to look at the extraordinary marine life of the coral beds; and Hué in the north, situated on a river the color of celadon called the Rivière des Parfums. Nhatrang was once an important city of the Cham dynasty and you still can see the seventh-century relics of those Hindu rulers, their ruined temples and decaying sanctuaries. The roofs rise in elaborate pyramids decorated with characteristic carving. The steep false arches, the narrow doorways and recessed pillars are all typical of this splendid vanished civilization.

Hué is practically in China. Capital of the Annamese empire of the nineteenth century, it was the Imperial City of the Son of the Celestial Empire. The Annamese emperor and his enormous retinue lived in the walled citadel on the bank of the river, and there you can find a dim echo of the Forbidden City in Peking—imperial palaces and pavilions with lacquered columns, doors painted with golden dragons, huge bronze urns flanking shallow stairways that lead to gardens and pools. At intervals the massive walls surrounding the citadel are punctuated by important gates, topped by more pavilions and living quarters for guards. These too, with their curling tile roofs decorated with rearing blue dragons, are entirely Chinese in conception and design.

A hundred years ago, with the arrival of the French, the three rival coastal kingdoms of Indo-China were united for the first time in an uneasy political unit. Until World War II French colonial rule maintained a watchful peace and Vietnam, which throughout its history had attracted traders and conquerors from all over Asia, found itself under European rule.

Now the Chinese came in a new invasion—not, this time, as military conquerors. In almost any town in Vietnam, you will find the shops, theatres, restaurants, pagodas and homes of the Chinese. In Saigon, they came in such large numbers that they established their own city, Cholon, meaning "big market," separated from Saigon only by a wide boulevard. Today Cholon is bigger in area and denser in population than Saigon; and most of the industry and commerce (except for the port traffic) is in Cholon.

Until the spring of 1955, when President Ngo Dinh Diem consolidated his power, Cholon had some of the best restaurants and night clubs (which hired French entertainers and imported shows from Paris). They were dominated by a fabulous, huge and sinister gambling den, the Grand Monde. People of every level of society—wealthy Chinese, an occasional Vietnamese official, foreigners in evening clothes, pedicab drivers, women with babies—indulged all night long in every known form of gambling from roulette to a puzzling Chinese game involving illuminated pictures moving across a small screen. The Grand Monde was run by the notorious chief of the Binh Xuyen sect, and was destroyed when he challenged President Diem's leadership in May, 1955. Diem, an austere Roman Catholic, who is a bachelor, has since warred on the "four scourges"—alcohol, opium, prostitution and gambling—and the Grand Monde has been used as a refugee center and market place.

Cholon has felt the effects of the "new" Vietnam more than any other area. Until independence, it was a glittering magnet of restaurants, brothels and opium dens, with a feverish Saturday-night atmosphere on which war-surrounded cities thrive. There was an exhilarating atmosphere of unpredictable danger. The big, expensive restaurants like the Arc en Ciel, with their fine Chinese and French food and Parisian floor shows, had heavy wire screens along the sidewalk. These were put up in the turbulent days to protect customers from stray hand grenades. (Today they are used to keep out the beggars, a persistent problem.) In the Grand Monde and Arc en Ciel night clubs, with their bands imported from the Philippines, acrobats and conjurors from Hong Kong, dancers from Spain and comedians from France, the tables were jammed with pleasure seekers. A regiment of slender girls in Chinese or Vietnamese clothes acted as hostesses, dance partners and companions. Next door to the Grand Monde was a Chinese theatre, and the dissonant clanging of Chinese theatrical music mixed strangely with the familiar strains of American jazz.

The night clubs and restaurants still do a steady business, mostly patronized by the hordes of official Americans stationed in Saigon. But Cholon's Chinese ebullience has definitely quieted down as a result of Diem's drive to "Vietnamize" the Chinese. As in most Southeast Asian countries, the hard-working Chinese are a minority group in Vietnam, but they have succeeded in gaining control of two-thirds of the nation's economy. And although many families have been in the country for centuries, almost none have become Vietnamese citizens. This past winter Diem decreed all local-born Chinese to be Vietnamese citizens and severely restricted their business life. As a result, the gaudy neon lights in Chinese characters were hauled down and replaced by painted Vietnamese signs in the streets of Cholon, and the tempo of Chinese life has perceptibly slackened.

North of the seventeenth parallel in the province of Tonkin, the territory of the Vietminh has not only been strongly affected by China, but has assimilated so much of Chinese civilization that it, in turn, has influenced the culture of the bigger country. It is sad that the American tourist cannot now, nor probably for some time to come, visit the north, for Hanoi, the capital, is called the most exuberant of Indo-China's coastal cities. Until the tenth century it was the capital of the Annam empire, but as it grew toward China it developed a truly Chinese talent for landscaping and designed remarkable gardens around a lake in the center of town. One of the great schools of Chinese landscape painting originated here, and Hanoi adaptations of Chinese forms are seen in the eighth- and tenth-century temples that are jammed among the modern houses of the city.

Hanoi's attraction lay in its great sense of identity, its cleanliness, its distinctive character. It has produced many of the
outstanding intellectuals of Indo-China, and boasts one of the
richest archaeological museums in Asia. Its special fame, a
uniquely beautiful pagoda built on a single column made from
an enormous tree trunk, was destroyed in the confusion after
the war. Now the city is quiet again, better disciplined than the
south, yet with something of the creative civilization you associate
with the main body of China.

Close to Hanoi is the bay commanded by the city of Haiphong.
This bay is so beautiful that, next to Angkor, it is considered the
greatest sight of Indo-China. Thousands of islands stud an
expanse of water almost a thousand square miles in area. Sail
in a sampan among the weird pyramids and columns rising out
of the bay, and you move eerily through rock tunnels that are
submerged at high tide, climb over multicolored seaweed to
reach dim and lovely grottoes and suddenly find yourself on the
edge of hidden, bright blue lakes. You dodge between fantastic
stalactites while your boatmen search for the nests of sea swal-
lows, that traditional Chinese delicacy. They tell you stories of
the gigantic sea serpents that are supposed to haunt these waters,
and point out wild sheep, boars and monkeys on the odd, rocky
islets, jeweled with quartz. But unfortunately, for the present
at least, the American traveler must make his judgments of the
country from southern Vietnam alone.

The hardest thing about trying to understand the new Vietnamese character is the people themselves. Unlike their Cambodian and Laotian neighbors, they seem remote, polite but
withdrawn, and, for the casual traveler, they are virtually in-
accessible. The best place to know them is Saigon, where at least
one or two aspects of their life can be shared and where an

64

occasional Vietnamese government official turns up at a "mixed" party.

You can eat Vietnamese food at some of the local restaurants and learn that Vietnam is one of the few Asian countries that considers salad an essential part of a meal. Great plates of raw vegetables—scallions, beet tops, coriander and spinach—are placed on the table along with chopped meat and eggs and a stack of very thin rice pancakes. Using chopsticks, you place a mixture of the meats and vegetables in the center of a rice cake, fold the cake and dip it into a sauce of dried fish and vinegar.

After dinner, you can go to a Vietnamese theater, where you will see a long, long play composed of dozens of very short scenes. The actors all wear gaudy costumes of satin, made even shinier with sequins and tinsel. In the old plays the stories and the acting are traditional and stylized, dealing with generals and emperors and their troubles, battles and loves. Raucous music and cymbals accompany the fights and duels, which are so highly formalized they have become a kind of dance. The more modern plays reveal the Vietnamese to be concerned largely with the problems of an orthodox society in contact with "Westernization" and a changing world—a girl wants to marry against her parents' wishes; a young man deserts his home and family for the attractions of city life.

Even foreigners with years of experience are conscious of the difficulty of making Vietnamese friends. Certainly part of the explanation lies in the uneasy emotional retreat of a people who have been made to feel inferior by a series of domineering outsiders: first, and for more than a thousand years of their history, by their Asian neighbors the Chinese and the Cambodians; later, more briefly but with considerable intensity, by the French. Culturally, there is very little that a Vietnamese can call his own

—a few minor folk arts, perhaps, a slight innovation in food or dress or art, and that is about all. At this particular moment in history, when the new idea of "Vietnamization" is being fostered in the country, when the people are trying to establish some kind of separate national identity, and when the memories of foreign arrogance are still fresh, it is not really surprising that the Vietnamese prefer to approach their contacts with foreigners with care and reticence.

Meanwhile, most of them are very busy trying to reconstruct their own lives and their country after fifteen years of incessant war.

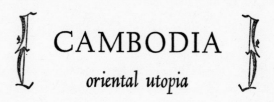

CAMBODIA
oriental utopia

IT SEEMS STRANGE THAT, WITHIN FOUR HOURS by car or jeep over rough roads, one can be in a country so different—historically, emotionally, and in its present conditions—as Vietnam is from Cambodia. I had been in Cambodia before, five years before, but in those days the guerrilla fighting in the jungles had been severe enough to close the land route between the two countries to anything but military travel. Of course, the plane flight had been even shorter than the drive and had deposited one in Pnom Penh, the capital of Cambodia, rather than in the border country, but this time our entry into Cambodia seemed to me more interesting both in mood and manner than our previous brisk flight. But in both cases certain obvious differences emerged. Cambodia suffered far less from the war than Vietnam. Having no major port, no industrial center, no cities of the size or importance of the Vietnamese cities of Saigon or Hanoi, having what the French describe as a "less industrious" people, Cambodia managed to maintain a high measure of disassociation from the war.

The fact that the Cambodians had a functioning royal tradition and an active king (the Vietnamese monarch, Bao Dai, had early in the conflict fled to France, where, to the great scorn of the nationalists, he maintained a life of moneyed leisure in French resorts), combined with the negative factor that with a smaller population and less productivity Cambodia was less useful to

France—less worth fighting about—saved the country from the devastation that Vietnam had seen. Besides this, Cambodia and Vietnam are historical enemies; the people are considerably different in temperament, and their interests and relations with the French differ. For these reasons the Cambodians were eager to set up their own separate government, to establish themselves as an independent state and pursue their special way of life.

We got a small glimpse of this change-over on our return to Cambodia because, by chance, a French friend of ours was there. He had been doing his two years of required service in the Indo-Chinese war, had been made a battalion commander and was currently stationed in a small Cambodian post called Snoul to supervise the transfer of power from the French to the Cambodians. He drove us, in his jeep, over the two hundred miles of dusty, bumpy road from Saigon to Snoul to stay for a few days with him at his battalion headquarters. During the first half of the drive we were constantly aware of the enormous military withdrawal. We were the only car going north; all the others seemed to be streaming single file down the road toward Saigon. Army lorries, jeeps, tanks and staff cars—chauffeured by everything from turbaned Moroccans to Foreign Legionnaires. The returning Zouaves in their giddy uniforms yelled from passing trucks, "Vive les coloniales!" For miles on end we rattled through the tropical countryside of flooded rice fields, farmers knee deep in the muddy water working to return their land to its old abundance, herds of water buffaloes tended by the small boys.

As we approached the Cambodian border the obvious signs of military occupation and war retreated, and we entered a sort of no-man's land of unreclaimed jungle. Except for elephants (which we saw once), and an infrequent naked aboriginal carry-

ing a primitive bow and a quiverful of arrows, we were alone in
an apparently deserted area. The only reminders of the recent
conflict were a narrow strip of what the French call *forêt
clairière,* or "medium dense jungle," cleared along the road as
a protection against ambush, and the sinister look of every sign-
post, milestone and road marker, perforated with bulletholes.

At the Cambodian border, by some mysterious geographical
alchemy, the color of the soil suddenly changes to a deep, bright
red. The Cambodians are superstitious about it—hate to farm
the brown soil, and feel that their own red earth has special
nationalistic properties and will always be returned to them.
The forests of "false teak" (a sort of unpleasant, imitative cousin
of real teak which looks, and, for a while, acts like teak, but if
you use it for building soon rots away) were replaced by the
great rubber plantations for which Cambodia was once so
highly prized by the French. Most of them were part of the
giant French combine, *Société des Plantations Terre Rouge,* but
now, so close to the border, after so many years of war and
neglect, they were simply vast, abandoned avenues, each tree
scarred with a spiral gash which used to ooze the precious milky
sap of rubber, but was now healed over with irregular black
scabs.

As we moved further into Cambodia, a difference in the atmosphere of the villages, a more cheerful, lackadaisical look about
the people, a greater sense of leisure simply in the way they
would stand at the side of the road and stare at the jeep, or talk
to us whenever we stopped for a drink or to stretch our legs,
made it clear that we had left the more tense and driven nature
of the Vietnamese behind. We arrived at last at Snoul to discover that our friend had arranged for us to stay in the house of
a rubber planter, long since returned to France. Set in the shade

of several giant acacia trees, surrounded by the dark green ranks of rubber trees, the house itself was big and cool with stone floors, high ceilings, deep verandahs covered with bougainvillaea. It was easy, there, to imagine the old, luxurious colonial days, dozens of servants, cool drinks on the verandah of an evening, with the hand-cranked gramophone playing dated French jazz.

We were to eat our meals with our friend in the officers' mess at battalion headquarters, and return each night to the planter's house, and this shuttling between the two provided a curiously appropriate background to an important moment in Southeast Asian history—the end of 350 years of colonialism. It was partly sad, partly triumphant. Every day in the officers' mess we would eat French food and drink French red wine (and learn the army slang for it, *rouquin* or *pousse au crime*). The menu would be written in violet ink on a sheet of white paper and the junior-most officer would read it aloud to the table, adding his own comments and cracks, ending, perhaps, with a *bon appetit* for everyone, and the wish that the senior officers should eat till they burst "because that is the only way we will ever be promoted in the French army now."

But every day there would be fewer officers at the table. Many had already left, and every morning brought a new batch of transfer orders for a few more. Almost every afternoon or evening there were small parties of celebration or farewell after the French had handed over to their Cambodian counterparts. At night, at dinner there would be small, formal presents offered to the battalion commander from the new Cambodian officers— usually glassy-looking dogmeat sausages, or the special rice cakes of the district, or buffalo steaks—clearly, the food in the officers' mess was going to change a great deal, very soon. Afterward we would go back to the great, empty, echoing house of the vanished planter.

Often in the evenings we would walk through the little village of Snoul with its few Chinese shops, a busy open-air restaurant with wooden benches and trestle tables set out on the unpaved road, some houses, a tailor, a place to mend bicycles, nothing very much, but with a nice, relaxed outgoing air about it, particularly at that soft hour of sunset when the people are back from the fields and the river. In the settlement of plantation workers (headed by Chinese foremen) we heard that work had already begun on the rubber plantations and would soon be expanding. Some arrangement had been made either to take over the French holdings, or to work the plantations under different management.

The last evening we were in Snoul, the Cambodian soldiers gave a dance for our friend, the battalion commander. He, too, had handed over command that day—the last to leave. The small orchestra of guitars and drums played the inevitable *lamtong* music. Some of the Cambodians already had their wives on the post and together they danced the hesitant, swaying steps. Others danced with fellow soldiers, or formed a long line, following the steps of the man in front. They drank beer and soda pop, and we sat a little apart drinking the cognac they had provided for us, trying to be part of the gaiety, but inevitably rather removed from it.

Early the next morning all three of us climbed back into the jeep to drive down to Saigon again, where we were to see our friend off on his plane back to Paris. It seemed a curiously flat departure. A couple of Cambodian officers to see us off and our friend's batman. A few wishes for a good journey. Had we got a bottle of wine against thirst on the dusty journey? Some bread? Sausage? Well . . . have a good trip. Well . . . good-by. I had to keep reminding myself that this was the end of an era, that the French were the last to relinquish their colonies in Asia. It is true that a few tiny pockets of colonialism remain—the British in Borneo, the Dutch in New Guinea, the Portuguese in Timor —but on the whole they are insignificant. With the withdrawal of the French from Indo-China, for the first time in centuries, Southeast Asia was free of foreign rule.

For a moment, in the jeep, I turned to look back at the battalion headquarters. The early-morning breeze had caught the flag at the top of its tall, unstable flagpole, a yellow elephant against a background of plain red, the Cambodian emblem. It had returned to its old, proud name of the Royal Khmer Army; its soldiers wore the golden insignia of the monkey god. We, with our French friend, turned back to watch the road taking us to Saigon.

If the modern Cambodian talent appears to be for a rather improbable prettiness in art, for a softly pleasing way of life—if, in fact, Cambodia seems to offer almost a ready-made setting for a theatrical extravaganza, it is a recent manifestation and in many ways misleading. At one time or another the country has governed an empire of five nations, raised an army of five million, built some of the most grandiose temples, palaces and cities in the world, and produced an art at once austerely beautiful and infinitely elaborate. It has been sacked and captured by conquering armies. Its cities have been destroyed, its treasures looted, its great monuments wrecked. It has painfully recaptured and welded into a national entity some of the lost provinces of its state. It has reinstated its royal line. And it is against this magnificent and tragic background that the lighthearted charm of the life in modern Cambodia must be set.

Yet it is tempting, when you first see the pastel pavilions of the royal palace in the capital, Pnom Penh, to think of Cambodia as a sort of musical-comedy country, and many things seem to support the atmosphere of charming frivolity. From the shiny green-and-yellow tiles of the roofs of the palace buildings, from the eaves of the dance pavilions and the storehouses of the royal treasures, slender curving snakes arch outward into the air with a grandiloquent flourish. Strangely insubstantial for the palace of a powerful monarch, they give the buildings the sense of being suspended from the pale Cambodian sky, rather than being built on solid foundations. Most of the pavilions are open on all four sides and passers-by may see the bright, inconsequential murals inside—celestial dancers, birds, trees, temples and people.

In the royal pagoda the floor is tiled with silver, and images of gold encrusted with diamonds are on display. There, too, are stylized murals—stiff, old-fashioned figures in mythological scenes or moments from the life of Buddha. These are constantly refurbished by local craftsmen; nothing is much more than thirty years old, and most of it is bright with gay decoration.

If you ever attend a royal banquet or a ceremony at the palace, the air of theatrical unreality will be intensified. Foreign ladies in wide tulle balldresses curtsy to the king, while his own people drop to their knees with palms pressed together in obeisance to their ruler. Most Cambodian court ladies stay in their quarters, and probably only one of the senior princesses will be present to join the elaborate retinue of the king's personal attendants. After dinner the king will lead his guests to one of the dance pavilions. The grounds and the façades of the buildings are illuminated with concealed floodlights. On each side of the procession courtiers carry flaming torches to throw a flickering light on the jewelry of the party. The king himself is flanked by equerries, official fanbearers and an attendant who holds a large green silk umbrella—the symbol of rank—over the royal head. (On important ceremonial occasions the king is sheltered by the full number of umbrellas to which his royal blood entitles him—nine of them rising one above the other in a fantastic pyramid.)

The dance pavilion is decorated with sprays of fresh flowers, and is perfumed with the faint and haunting scent of the night jasmine.

After the first arresting notes from the musicians, the royal dancers appear, wearing the fabulously rich and dramatic costumes that have been traditionally theirs for generations. The characteristic headdresses, rising in slender spires of gold, are studded with huge diamonds, rubies and emeralds. On their upper arms, wrists and ankles, around the neck and waist, are more jewels magnificently set in many designs. The close-fitting costumes glitter with brocade, gold paillettes, silver thread and the luster of heavy hand-woven silk.

They glide through the complex patterns of the dances, fingers incredibly curling backward like the petals of a tiger lily, recounting the ancient legends of kings and queens, of loves and abductions, of battles and victories. The dances and the dancers are traditionally a part of the court of Cambodia, the formal and necessary entertainment offered by the king to his guests or his subjects. And they are one of the most impressive links between modern and ancient Cambodia. Poses from their dances are carved on monuments a thousand years old; their costumes and the stories of their dances are souvenirs of the far-flung international contacts Cambodia once had. Their jewelry and their gold headdresses are reminders of a vanished royal wealth so great that it could not be assessed.

I attended such a royal party one night. This was before the present king had accepted the throne from his abdicating son, which enabled the younger man, as simply a prince of Cambodia, to become its constitutional elected prime minister. One of the king's ministers turned to me, and, gesturing toward the king in a white-and-gold uniform sitting in his gilt chair, his round, slightly smiling face turned to the stage, the assembled courtiers and foreign dignitaries, he asked, "Do you have such ceremonies in Indian palaces?"

I replied that while we still have maharajas in India, very few of them have permanent court dancers.

He looked rather shocked at the idea of so pedestrian a royalty. "Here," he told me with some emphasis, "it is both the prerogative and the duty of the king to protect our arts. The queen mother personally supervises the training of the dancers. Because she is a scholar and an artist our dancing is not lost. It is a great honor for a girl to be chosen to become a dancer. Tonight you will even see the king's daughter performing with the royal ballet."

When the dancing began I understood why the Cambodian ballet is considered among the court treasures, as valuable as the fabulous jewelry, as distinctive as the royal insignia.

Today His Majesty Suramarit Norodom, King of Cambodia and Supreme Head of its Buddhist religion, rules over a country of about four million people situated on the Indo-Chinese peninsula between Thailand and Vietnam. His ancestry reaches back into legendary times when Queen Willow Leaf, a descendant of the moon, ruled her paradisiacal realm alone until a

Brahmin arrived from India. First he was horrified that the queen and her subjects wore no clothes; then, as a generous gesture, he gave her some material and showed her how to drape herself modestly. Finally, setting what came to be a historic pattern, he succumbed to the enchantment of the country, married Queen Willow Leaf and made Cambodia his home.

From this legendary origin there grew a race of rulers who, sometimes arrogantly, and sometimes with desperation, held on to Cambodia through many hundreds of years, clinging to the customs of their land.

The earliest accounts of Cambodian life come from indefatigable Chinese who, centuries ago, journeyed all over Asia, and wrote letters home with astonishing energy. One such report dates from the fourth century and tells of the Cambodian conversion to Brahminism and describes the Cambodians as worshiping "the Spirits of Heaven," and carving religious images. "Those with two faces have four arms, and those with four faces have eight arms." In the temples that were constructed five centuries later, you can see these same images carved in stone, corroded by the jungle, in the ancient deserted cities of Cambodia. And even today, in the royal entourage of the King of Cambodia, there are always three Brahmins who officiate at certain ceremonies even though the state religion for centuries has been Buddhism.

In the fifth century the King of Cambodia (known to the Chinese then as Funan) asked the Chinese Emperor for help in subduing a neighboring king who governed what is now the coast of Vietnam, and described his enemy as "a miserable criminal." Today, in the great bas-reliefs of the crumbling palaces of Angkor, you can read the legends of those ancient battles, observe the armor of the warriors—the spears, axes, crossbows and

78

shields—the chariots and horses, the oxen and elephants. In any Cambodian village you will find oxcarts that have changed little in design from their ancient models; the small boys shoot at birds with identical homemade crossbows; and driving on a Cambodian jungle road you may find an elephant blocking your way.

A couple of hundred years later, one of Funan's vassal states led a rebellion against the king, conquered the country and founded what must have been the first Khmer kingdom—the people who were eventually to build Cambodia's greatest wonders. Early in the ninth century a great ruler, Jayavarman II, "rose like a fresh lotus," ruled the Khmer empire for fifty years and began the building of the incredible city of Angkor which even today—in ruins, devoured by the jungle—remains one of the world's greatest artistic and architectural achievements.

For four centuries, from their capital city Angkor, the Khmers dominated all of Southeast Asia. As their power grew they ruled Siam and the Indo-Chinese states and received tribute from the Malay peninsula and Sumatra. In the picture history carved on the walls of Angkor you see the slave labor exacted from the conquered people. But the Angkorean period was both the height and the finish of the Khmers.

In an outburst of Brahmin and later Buddhist fervor, the Khmer kings built temples, shrines and tombs in which they worshiped their gods and by a curious substitution deified themselves. In the strange and haunting temple of Bayon, for instance, at the center of the royal city, those long-ago Khmers saw in the huge, half-smiling stone faces gazing out from every tower, both the image of Lokesvara, the Compassionate Buddha, and also the semidivine features of their king, watching over the distant provinces of his realm. By the thirteenth century, Jayavarman VII, the last of the great "constructor-kings," brought to an almost frenzied pitch this mania for building. Some historians suggest this was because he was a leper and hoped to flatter the gods into curing him. Some say he hoped for an eternal reward.

Whatever the reason, the construction of the hundreds of buildings that are still scattered through the Cambodian jungle around Angkor—the acres of carving, the thousands of statues —ruined his people and ended his kingdom. Great armies of slaves carried the slabs of sandstone and laterite from miles around to build the royal city. Countless artisans, artists and sculptors gave their lives in this frantic chiseling. In the end the kingdom was, literally, exhausted.

For a long time historians assumed that the Khmer race was totally destroyed after Jayavarman VII's reign; and certainly there was a kind of terrible drama in the fact that an entire people, after creating one of the world's wonders, disappeared from the face of the earth. One theory suggested that some cosmic justice operated to change the course of the rivers and force a decimating migration on a people who had expended the lives of their subject peoples with such abandon. However, new archaeological discoveries make it seem more probable that the great kingdom of the Khmers simply pushed itself into a period of decadence and war, so that effective resistance to outside attacks became impossible.

Quickly Cambodia's neighbors saw their advantage. From the fourteenth century on it was repeatedly attacked. Siam looted the treasures of its temples and even now some of the best of Khmer art is in the Bangkok museum. The Cambodian dances and dancers were carried away to the court of Siam. Meanwhile from the east, the coastal nation of Annam and the armies of Cochin China swept over the dwindling kingdom of Cambodia, seizing its gold and leaving Angkor to decay in the jungle.

For the visitor to Angkor now, this mottled history has left an enthralling legacy—the vast and beautiful ruins, and a haunting mystery. Of all the marvelous and lovely things to be seen in Angkor, the greatest is generally accepted to be the temple Angkor Vat itself. Larger than any temple in India, it is built on the traditional Hindu design of a huge outer wall and galleries set on a rectangular plan, and enclosing rectangular courtyards and buildings of diminishing size. Around the outer galleries, on their miles of wall space are carved in incredible detail the bas-reliefs which illustrate the stories from the great Hindu epics. The vitality and expertise of these carvings are so impressive—huge, lumbering elephants tricked out in the fantastic panoply of war, cavalry charges and foot soldiers, lavish court scenes or the daily life in the royal city, demons and gods and jungle animals—that it seems impossible that there could have been so many brilliant craftsmen all at work on the same monument at the same moment in history.

Within these outer galleries, which are, perhaps, Angkor Vat's greatest wonder, are dozens of partly-ruined buildings. Some were subsidiary temples and shrines, some were libraries, some places of meditation, and some dance pavilions. In fact, music and dance are so intimate a part of Hinduism that many of the pavilions and galleries, hundreds of lintels, pillars and niches are decorated with countless figures and poses of dancers and musicians. Those infinitely graceful women, improbably slender of waist and full-breasted, loaded with jewelry but covered with only a few clinging folds of diaphanous material, their hair wound in elaborate coiffures and held with pearls and flowers, a faint, secret smile on their lips, dance out at you from doorways and dark corners, catch your eye as you walk down a corridor, or appear, sharply modeled in sunlight, on the outer wall of a temple. It is easy to see why the tradition of court dancers has never disappeared from Cambodia.

The innermost shrine of Angkor Vat rises in a steep and heavily decorated pyramid at the heart of the great temple. If you have the courage to climb the vertiginous steps and reach the austere chambers and passages that must have been the sanctum of those ancient priests, you can look out between the pillars and see below you the immense complex of buildings that make up Angkor Vat, the beautifully proportioned courtyards, the endless imagination that went into the designing of the columns —no two alike—the paved and sunken spaces between shrines that were probably, at one time, sacred bathing pools, the nobility of the plan, contrasted with the meticulous detail of the decoration, and the oddly satisfying combination of the somber gray stone peculiar to Angkor and the exuberant, sunlit green of the jungle around it.

Behind you will be the narrow, dark stone chamber that once held the image of the chief deity. It will smell of bats and seem inexplicably simple compared with the vibrant sculpture and decoration around it. Now that Hinduism has been replaced by Buddhism in Cambodia, many of the shrines and niches that held the old Brahminic symbols and deities are filled with statues of Buddha, and through the caverns of shadow in Angkor Vat and the striped light of the galleries, on the long stone causeways and on the steep staircases you will see the brilliant yellow robes of Buddhist priests, each with his begging bowl in one hand and the ubiquitous umbrella in the other.

Next to Angkor Vat itself, I suppose the most imposing and unusual sight in the six hundred ruined buildings of the ancient capital (only six hundred have been reclaimed from the jungle so far; evidently there are many more still overgrown and undiscovered) is Bayon, the chief temple of the royal city of Angkor-Thom. Nothing of the sort now exists in its parent culture of India. Around Bayon are the evocative ruins of a whole lost way of life—immense stone terraces, and huge throne platforms from which perhaps the Khmer kings used to review their troops, the crumbling remains of a palace, of a convent, some structures that one can no longer identify, with the tall white-boled trees that the French call *fromager* growing through gaping roofs and winding sinuous roots around pillars and pavements, an elephant-mounting platform, memorial statues, private shrines, proud triumphal gateways, elegant bridges and avenues—but Bayon itself dominates all of Angkor-Thom.

Bayon has fifty towers, lichened, decaying, but still rising with astonishing authority above the steamy muddle of the jungle. On each side of each tower is carved an enormous, enigmatic face of the ancient God-king, half-smiling, watchful, powerful, an intimidating and unforgettable sight. I remember Bayon best from an occasion, years ago, when we drove out to the ruin in an army truck with a group of friends—French soldiers who were being sent to the front the next day. There had been a good deal of rather desperate celebration that night, much drinking of coarse red wine and toasts to distant sweethearts in France, many nostalgic songs about *"Mon Village au Claire de Lune,"* and *"J'ai Deux Amours, Mon Pays et Paris."* We reached Bayon before the full moon cleared the jungle and scrambled out of the truck, still laughing and singing, to climb the wide steps and walk the paved path toward Bayon. As we reached the first terrace, the moon appeared over the tops of the trees, and suddenly those hundreds of calm, knowing, tolerant faces, grayish-white in the moonlight, subtly shadowed, stared out at us from the towers of Bayon. We all stopped—stopped talking, laughing and singing, stopped walking—and stared back, caught for a moment in the fugitive magic of the dead Khmer empire.

But of all the magnificent buildings in Angkor, the palaces, fountains, temples, colleges, my particular favorite is a small temple, tiresome to reach (by jeep over bad roads), late in date and recently reconstructed, called Banteay Srei. Henri Marchal, the French archaeologist who was responsible for its reconstruction, calls it a "carved jewel," and in fact, when you first see it, it does convey all the tiny, compact beauty of a ruby; the sculpture has the meticulous precision of a faceted precious stone.

It is built in a rose-pink sandstone, dedicated to Parvati, the consort of the Hindu god Shiva, and, appropriately enough, manages to distill in its shrines and pavilions the essence of elegant femininity. The over-all design is the conventional rectangular one on an almost miniature scale, but the special loveliness of Banteay Srei is in its carvings and decorations. Each of the hundreds of poses of Parvati with her attendants, dressing, being adorned with jewels, in moments of affection with the Lord Shiva, as a goddess, as a woman—each one is an individual and exquisite work of art. The decorations over the doors and on the pillars of balustrades have a particular, almost finicky delicacy, curling, elaborate, unimaginably expert. Compared with the gray, imposing stature of the great buildings of Angkor, Banteay Srei provides a moment of charm, lightness and a pastel beauty.

It wasn't until the middle of the last century that Cambodia, aided by the French, pushed back the invaders and re-established its sovereignty. France forced the Siamese to return the sacred sword, symbol of kingly power, to the royal house of Norodom. Cambodia's richest territory, its fisheries, its most productive rice-lands and the ruins of Angkor were wrested from the Siamese. A Cambodian king came to the throne in a new capital. Once again he held court, conferred with his ministers, patronized his royal dancers and began the curious process of reviving a country that had barely escaped extinction. Almost a hundred years later, his great-grandson saw yet another foreign invader—the Japanese —give three of his provinces to Siam as a reward for collabora-tion in World War II. In 1946 he received those provinces back and resumed his rule of the country under a loose protectorate arrangement with the French. However, he was certain enough of his royal power to decide early in 1953 that Cambodia should be entirely independent. To force the decision from the French he went into exile, announcing that he wouldn't return unless his demands were met. The French apparently recognized his power and the hold of royalty on the Cambodians, for the matter was settled shortly and the king returned as independent ruler of Cambodia, the first in five hundred years. More recently still, in yet another show of independence, that young king abdicated to become a politician and to lead the country now as prime minister while his father rules it as king.

The vast maneuverings of kings and empires or armies and politicians affect most of the people hardly at all. This is some-thing to remember about Asia. Times are good or bad, crops are rich or poor, a war may take away some of the young men, an invader may levy a new tax—but in the big context of life in the villages and on the land things move along in pretty much the same way. Very occasionally in Asian history you get a man who genuinely catches the imagination of the people—a Buddha or a Gandhi—and his power is incalculable; but for the most part there is a sort of indestructibility to the attitude and pattern of Asian village life.

Therefore, it is in the villages that you find the character and appeal of the people. But you must be willing to cope with them on something approximating their own terms, and to travel without making comfort a prime object. There is only one railway in Cambodia and it connects the capital with the Siamese border. Airlines take you from Pnom Penh to Siemreap, the small town closest to the ruins of Angkor, but all the rest of your travel has to be by bus along fairly rough roads; or, best of all, by river boats.

To the Cambodians the great river Mekong represents about the same in legend and agricultural wealth as the Ganges does to Indians. It rises in Tibet and flows south along the Laos-Thailand border and through Cambodia to the China Sea. In addition to water and water power it offers a means of communication and provides a bounty of fertile soil. The greatest festivals are connected with the Mekong, the liveliest village life is along its banks and those of its tributaries, and the thought of the Mekong is what makes Cambodians, when abroad, most homesick.

The Mekong makes the countryside rich, self-sufficient and rather leisurely. Twice a year it floods and conveniently irrigates the rice paddies. Also, the Mekong is full of fish which the Cambodians catch in a uniquely easy way: they dig holes in the bank just before the river rises, and when it recedes the holes are full of fish. Twice a year the village fish supply is replenished, and quantities are dried for future meals.

Every two or three miles along the Mekong and its tributaries there is a little village surrounded by coconut palms and fruit trees—papayas, bananas, *chikoos*, sweet limes, jack fruit—the usual abundance of the tropics. Here and there are ragged-topped areca palms, the neater outlines of toddy palms, and trellises of betel vines. For every village there is a temple with its steep roof shining in the sun. At wider intervals are Cambodia's chief towns, with Chinese shops and restaurants, and with more elaborate water fronts.

The pleasantest way to see the Cambodian countryside and visit with its people is to take a trip on a river boat, adjusting to the slow pace of life, sharing the food and the interests of the natives. From Kompong Cham, Cambodia's chief commercial town, to the capital Pnom Penh is, for instance, an eight-hour boat ride (two hours by car) and it costs about fifty cents with an extra twenty-five cents for a deck chair. You leave Kompong Cham around eight in the morning, although, of course, the boat will wait for you if you are late. All the other passengers will be intensely inquisitive about who you are and where you are going and why. As in all of Asia such questions are not considered rude and the people who ask them will be delighted to tell you in return, say, when they were married, how many children they have and whether they quarrel with their in-laws.

On the boat there will almost certainly be a couple of Chinese men neatly dressed in Western-style clothes, probably small businessmen or clerks. (The Cambodians have little business sense and not much interest in making money.) Most of your fellow passengers will be Cambodians. The women wear black sarongs with loose blouses, and bracelets or rings of the dark Cambodian silver beautifully worked in complicated designs. Their hair is cropped short in the style recently smart in Europe and America, but to them it is the conventional, old-fashioned coiffure. When a Cambodian woman covers her head she uses a straight piece of cloth and with a couple of almost thoughtless twists transforms it into a very stylish turban. One way and another, in spite of teeth often blackened with years of betel chewing, Cambodian women have an air of chic, and half the time it will be a woman who starts the conversation with a stranger.

A Cambodian friend of mine, a widow, once told me, "A Cambodian looks at the ground only before a priest or the king." Recently, when I saw her again after six years, we sat on the floor of her village house in the usual way, and drank coconut milk. Suddenly she announced that she had married again. "He is good to look at and much younger, but not very clever at earning money." She added casually, "I have had to open a small shop." She pointed out to me a store of soft drinks and cigarettes at the back.

I didn't know whether to commiserate or approve.

"Cambodian women are strong," she explained kindly, "and I am pleased with the arrangement. After my daughters found husbands, the house was too empty."

The men on the river boat are somewhat more retiring. They crouch on the deck, wearing checked cotton sarongs and no shirt, surrounded by the usual covey of small children in odd fragments of tattered shorts or sarongs. And usually there will be four or five shaven-headed Buddhist priests on board, in yellow robes draped to leave one shoulder bare.

You quickly see that religion is important in Cambodia and that great deference is shown the priests. Out of its population of about 4,000,000, nearly 100,000 men are priests or monks, and a large number of women—again with heads shaved, but dressed in white robes—are nuns. All live entirely on the charity of the faithful. On the river boat you notice that the Cambodian passengers do not eat until food is given to the priests aboard, and every time they pass where the priests sit, they fold their hands in a gesture of respect.

As the boat fills up, the atmosphere becomes more lively. People squat around your deck chair with baskets and bundles, and usually one of them who speaks a little French—often a child who has learned it at school—will interpret for you. All day the boat zigzags slowly downriver, stopping at villages every half hour or so. Passengers get on or off, sacks of rice or vegetables are loaded or unloaded. There is the inevitable exchange of news yelled out from boat to shore. Girls bathing in the river, their sarongs slicked becomingly to their bodies, shake the water from their hair and listen to the latest happenings in Kompong Cham. Women scrubbing clothes at the water's edge, children flopping happily about like eels in the shallows, all stop to stare and call out remarks and questions. Then, with an important scream of the ship's siren, you fuss off down the river once more.

At one village halfway through the morning a fleet of tiny pirogues, each propelled by a boy standing in the stern with one oar, skims out to meet the river boat. A dozen little girls clamber on board, each with covered baskets, and wander among the passengers, offering a variety of foods—cubes of lean meat on bamboo skewers coated with a reddish spicy sauce and still hot from the charcoal grills; neat little packages wrapped in banana leaves which contain a mixture of rice and vegetables seasoned with the delicious pepper for which Cambodia is famous; small fish—five on a skewer—salted and broiled; and bananas—fried, roasted, salted and spiced and cooked as a vegetable. Besides all this there are other fruits, slices of sugar cane and lumps of pickled garlic. Also, there is the inevitable array of the ingredients for betel chewing—the shiny green, heart-shaped leaves coated with lime and filled with areca nut, tobacco, cloves and cardamom, which are chewed after a meal as an aid to digestion, an astringent for the mouth, and to calm the mind.

In between the settlements on the Mekong are the landscapes of rice fields and palms. Once your eye is accustomed to this characteristic background of Southeast Asia, no other landscape is ever quite so pleasing, and forever in the back of your mind will remain the penetrating green of young rice, the grace of white herons moving over the paddies, the reds and browns of earth and river, the clear surprising yellow of the priests' robes along the country paths. Here and there the rice fields alternate with tidy avenues of rubber trees on the big French plantations, but in the end your eye will always come back with a pleasant sense of familiarity to the paddies and palms, the small shabby villages and the river.

By the time you reach Pnom Penh you will feel as though you had been friends all your life with your fellow passengers and you will have learned a lot about Cambodia.

Perhaps the most typically Cambodian moment of the year is usually sometime in November when the *Fête des Eaux* is held in Pnom Penh, for on that day all the things dearest to Cambodians are represented.

The festival concerns, inevitably, the Mekong, one of whose branches curiously flows one direction for half the year and in the opposite direction for the other half, and the *Fête des Eaux* celebrates the moment of its change. Naturally, religious ceremonies accompany the fete, and it is, besides, an occasion to pay tribute to the king, by whose command, traditionally, the waters change their direction.

Cambodians feel close to their monarch in a cozy, personal way. At the *Fête des Eaux* when everyone who can manage to get a boat rows out into the Mekong and past the floating pavilion where the king sits to watch the festivities, any Cambodian may call out from his pirogue, directly to the king, whatever problem is on his mind. Theoretically the king's advisers, sitting beside him, take notice of the matter and act to correct grievances.

The big moment of the day, however, delights the Cambodian's sense of spectacle with a royal magnificence. The king's festival boats appear on the river, each with a high curving prow of carved, gilded and painted wood. A hundred bare-chested oarsmen in bright sarongs stand in the dozens of boats. The king's pennants flutter from the floating pavilion. Before wildly cheering crowds the royal boat races begin. Late into the night the excitement continues, with fireworks, dancing and gambling. And then, at last, after the *Fête des Eaux*, the Cambodians settle back to their country life punctuated occasionally by a lesser fete, a market day, a temple ceremony, but mostly the numerous but quiet activities of life in a Cambodian village.

LAOS
land of leisure

NORTH OF CAMBODIA IS ONE OF THE FEW
"never-never lands" left anywhere in the world. Laos is charming,
absurd, beautiful and utterly removed from reality—for that, if
for nothing else, in these days of strain and anxiety it should be
cherished. When we were in Cambodia we inquired about how
we could get to Laos. Someone told us, rather doubtfully, "Well,
you *could* go up by river—of course it *does* take a very long time."

"Oh, that doesn't matter," I replied blithely. "We're in no
hurry."

"Better ask the river boatmen; they'll know."

Well, you *can* get to Laos by the River Mekong—*if* you are
there at the right moment when the river is navigable that far up,
if you have several weeks to spend chugging upstream in a
variety of small boats, *if* at the border you are prepared to get out
and make your own way around the rapids, and *if* after that you
can make arrangements to continue with Laotian boatmen. We
didn't go by boat. We took a plane and the journey lasted only
a couple of hours. But I have always rather regretted that we
didn't attempt the river trip; the country would certainly have
been beautiful, and it seems like exactly the right, fantastic way
to approach Laos.

Landlocked, by geography, in the heart of the Indo-Chinese
peninsula, with borders on China and northern Vietnam, and
pleasantly remote by nature, the Laotians were less affected by

the Indo-Chinese war than any other part of the country. There is a kind of fortuitous justice in this because the Laotians are among the very few people in the world that have never fought an aggressive war. They are far from simple, but, in this over-complicated world, they have managed to retain a sure touch on the fundamentals of living and a miraculously unruffled approach to life.

A story concerns the visit some years ago of a French Minister for the Colonies. The minister arrived full of a scheme to give the colonies the same eight-hour work day that the French enjoyed at home. In Tonkin and Annam—provinces of Vietnam—where overpopulation had created everything from sweatshop conditions to child labor, the new regulation was greeted with enthusiasm. In Cambodia it was met with some surprise because it had never occurred to the Cambodians to work more than eight hours a day. But in Laos it was received with horrified protest. "Eight hours?" the Laotians cried. "What do the French want—slave labor?"

Now, of course, Laos is an independent state and can formulate its own laws, can at last develop its own large and untapped resources. It has come uneasily into focus for many people who had never heard of it before because it shares two of its boundaries with Communist territories and seems like an obvious and un-guarded area for Communist penetration. But even today you will hear stories about its *sang-froid* from foreigners in Laos who attribute the Laotians' unhurried life variously to malnutrition, fatigue, a wiser philosophy and plain indolence. Actually, none of these theories is entirely satisfactory, for Laos is an extremely rich and virtually unexploited country. There is usually plenty of food for everybody. It is the second largest of the nations that make up Indo-China and it has the smallest population—about a million and a half. But while the Laotian's diet of rice, fish and fruit keeps him healthy, he cultivates only the amount of land necessary to maintain himself and his family. Nor is it true that a Laotian *never* works hard; in fact, before a festival most of the men are busily carving new decorations for the temples, or building bamboo pavilions and decorating them with flowers and foliage, while the women cook special food and make rice wine. And they aren't really so tired, because they stay up all night gambling, watching boxing matches and wandering around the nighttime bazaars set up for the fete. It is just that the Laotians are not particularly ambitious, and this is probably harder than anything else for the visiting Westerner to understand.

Foreigners in Laos tell you that if you want to get anything done—a house built or an office run efficiently—you must hire Vietnamese. The Laotians, as often as not, placidly agree; even for their festivals they hire Siamese to put on boxing matches. Of course, there *are* Laotian boxers, but they prefer to watch other people exert themselves. The complicated night-long dramas that Laotians love are nearly always acted by a troupe from one of their neighbor countries, and the gambling booths are run by Chinese. It is the Laotians who enjoy themselves, who are amused by the entertainment, excited by the gambling and delighted by the festival.

After a short while in the country you find that the Laotian way of doing things is both pleasant and contagious. Increasingly you use the Laotians' favorite phrase, *"bo pen yan"*—meaning roughly "It doesn't really matter." You are enchanted by a hospitality so inclusive that a Laotian, before he sits down to dinner with his guests, says, *"soen-soen,"* meaning, "I invite you," which is directed not only to those who are there by appointment but to whoever may happen to be passing on the street or standing in the garden. You are charmed by the courtesy you find everywhere, and you become so accustomed to utter honesty that, like the Laotians, you leave your valuables lying about and never lock your house.

Why Laos should have developed this appealing and unruffled character is rather hard to determine. Certainly its geography has helped by providing fertile soil and a relatively comfortable climate; but its history should have produced a more wary and a fiercer nation. The Laotians, however, have paid little attention to their history. Virtually no records were kept before the thirteenth century, and even the later manuscripts were scratched on leaves and carelessly left about to be destroyed by weather or termites. However, from old monuments, from the religion, the language and the people themselves, certain things are clear. One is that the great empire of the Khmers, which flourished in Cambodia on the southern borders of Laos from the ninth to the thirteenth centuries, spread Brahminism and later Buddhism to Laos, and left its influence on Laotian art. From the jewelry, the dances, the architecture, you can see that in the following centuries there was considerable exchange with Siam. And at one time or another China has pushed southward to Laos too.

None of these influences were entirely peaceful. The Khmers conquered the northern Laotian provinces. The armies of Kublai Khan later considered Laos a vassal state. From the fourteenth to the sixteenth centuries, at the cost of a number of wars with Burma and Annam, Laos held a brief and shaky independence under a succession of strong kings. But in the seventeenth and eighteenth centuries Laos again was annexed, this time by its western and eastern neighbors, Siam and Annam. Twice the royal city of Luang Prabang was burned, its people enslaved and its treasures looted—including the emerald Buddha, now in Bangkok.

Only sixty years ago, under a French protectorate, Laos again acquired a sort of sovereignty even though a large slice of its territory remained part of Siam, and most of its people are now officially Siamese. The French administered the country with only the thinnest attempt at co-operation, but the Laotians didn't seem to mind, and nowadays one hears far less bitterness about the days of French colonialism in Laos than in other parts of Indo-China.

In spite of such a long and recent history of conquest and annexation, the Laotians took the matter calmly when their royal city was threatened last year by the troops of the Vietminh. When the French insisted that the Laotians prepare for the defense of their city, spokesmen pointed out that Luang Prabang had been named for the small golden image of Buddha in the royal pagoda, Prabang, and it was its duty to protect the city. Why should the citizens be so arrogant as to take on the duties of the gods? The Buddhist priests increased their prayers and some of the people of Luang Prabang performed acts of devotion, but for the most part life continued as usual. When the situation became really critical foreign paratroopers from other parts of Indo-China were rushed to Laos and after some bitter fighting the advance was halted just a few kilometers outside the city. The Laotians' bland acceptance of the rescue should have come as no surprise to the French, but a French friend of mine who was there at the time said that he never thought up a suitable answer to the frequent Laotian comment, "You see, there was no reason to worry. Prabang protected us after all."

Probably the best place in Laos to learn the special flavor and pace of Laotian life is in the royal capital of Luang Prabang itself. The French capital in the south, Vientiane, however, is more accessible. Its undistinguished buildings housing the government offices and foreign legations on avenues deeply shaded by acacias and huge teak trees, its private homes of a French colonial style or the airy wooden houses raised on stilts, common to all Indo-China, stretch along the River Mekong, the boundary with Siam. Here some of the vigorous habits of the Thais have penetrated, and in the mornings the essential work of running a government gets accomplished. However, even in Vientiane, one is often reminded that Laos functions according to rules of its own. When I was there, for instance, the prime minister and his cabinet resigned, but for weeks on end nobody formed a new government; or else you learn that a good deal of quiet smuggling goes on from Siam—such unexpected items as fresh vegetables; not because one can't grow vegetables in Laos, but for some reason it seems simpler to bring them across the Mekong at night. But Vientiane still carries something of the atmosphere of the French, while in Luang Prabang, the only other city of any size in the country, you are really in the heart of Laos.

Luang Prabang is set—with a great eye for the beauty of the country and with no sense of convenience—at the meeting of the Mekong with one of its tributaries. All around it rise the high misty mountains of the north. There are no trains in Laos; the road from the south is impassable for much of the year and there is no road from the north; the Mekong, which provides a slow but convenient waterway within the country, develops some treacherous rapids at the Cambodian border that effectively disqualify the river as a means of international communication. The simplest way to get to Luang Prabang is by plane—if the rains are over and if the town's encircling mountains are free enough of cloud to allow your pilot to find the air strip. The narrow tongue of land on which Luang Prabang is built is almost an island and even when you land at the airport you still must wait around for a ferry to take you across the river to the town itself. But all this contributes to Luang Prabang's special and endearing atmosphere—its isolation, its beauty and its indifference to the rest of the world.

Under the royal Laotian flag—a three-headed elephant sheltered by an umbrella on a scarlet ground—the pleasant, white-washed buildings and curling roofs of the king's palace form the focus of the town. Opposite the palace, by some odd geological upheaval, there is a sharply rising pinnacle crowned by the sacred pagoda of Phu-si containing an imprint of the foot of Buddha. Around these two landmarks the clean and narrow streets of Luang Prabang spread in geometric patterns down to the water. There are a couple of restaurants, a small hotel, the unpretentious stucco houses of some of the noblemen and courtiers and the simpler wooden homes of the ordinary townspeople and, eventually, at the rivers' edges on every side of the town, the little shacks, the small piers and the countless pirogues of the boatmen.

There are few shops, but on the important market days the main streets of the town are lined with women who offer for sale some of the most beautiful silks and brocades in Asia. Hand-woven on narrow, old-fashioned looms in tiny homes, the Laotian silks have extraordinary and luminous colors—a green the color of parakeets; a glowing, changing blue like the feathers of a kingfisher; scarlets and yellows and the palest imaginable pink, as well as other more subtle hues produced by mixing the various silks. Many of the materials have gold or silver threads worked in stylized designs to form a border along the edge of the cloth; some have a silver thread woven in a scarcely discernible stripe all through the material, and the more elaborate are practically solid, shimmering metal. The most magnificent brocades of all are those made in the royal silk-weaving villages where experts weave especially for the king and the royal retinue.

At market time you also see the slender Meo tribesmen who have walked to town from the hills to barter for their needs. From the airplane on your way to the capital you see the tiny clearings on the crests of the hills, like bald spots, where the Meo people build their villages in seemingly impenetrable jungle. In Luang Prabang they look like foreigners in their distinctive clothes— loose, dark blue trousers and blouses tied tightly at the waist with wide sashes. Both men and women wear the typical heavy jewelry of wide loops of silver around the neck, and charms and amulets, and almost all of them have long hair casually knotted high on the back of the head. Most of the Meo men wear opium belts, strong bands of canvas with pockets sewn in. Here they carry the precious powder which they have extracted from the poppies they cultivate in their remote mountains and plateaus. For centuries this has brought them a furtive wealth.

Market days in Luang Prabang are brightened by teams of five or six elephants marching into town loaded with rice or bamboo. Stepping carefully around market stalls, avoiding merchandise spread out on the sidewalks, waiting patiently to be unloaded, these elephants are an essential part of the town's life. In fact, if you have the time and a strong enough stomach, you can persuade the elephant catchers of Luang Prabang to take you out trapping. You must allow yourself to be smeared with elephant dung to hide your odor, and march into the jungle with a decoy female elephant, to find a herd. And you must watch calmly while the decoy separates the young bulls, and then leads them back to captivity.

With much less effort, you can occasionally see a ceremony for which the king's royal elephants are led into town, forty of them, painted with flowers and abstract designs, decorated with silver and gold elephant jewelry, ridden by silk-dressed royal elephant keepers who live in special villages.

To me the most pleasing sight in Luang Prabang is the Laotian women of the north going about their daily chores, shopping, strolling, selling their cloth. Smiling slightly, friendly, a little curious, they have a special and arresting grace, a remarkable air of precise elegance; and they have evolved one of the most beautiful costumes in Asia. A Laotian woman uses a straight length of heavy, beautiful native silk to form her skirt. She wraps it tightly about her hips, fastens it at the waist with a belt of gold or silver links, and allows it to reach a length that for Asia is daringly short—just above the middle of her calf. Her bodice is also a length of silk, matching or blending but not necessarily identical with her skirt. She binds this around her body from her waist up to cover her breasts, and one end of the material, usually fringed or decorated, is thrown over her right shoulder to hang down her back, leaving her left shoulder bare.

Her silks may be very simple, with practically no gold or silver; or they may have just a narrow decorative border around the hem of the skirt, or they may be the heaviest and richest brocades. Her choice is usually determined by the time of day, the occasion, and her economic status. Probably she will have made all or part of her costume herself, for weaving is an essential part of a Laotian girl's education.

Along with its beautiful women, Luang Prabang's other pride is its pagodas. In everything else the Laotians prefer simplicity, but their pagodas show an astonishing energy. In and around Luang Prabang there are about seventy pagodas, some extravagantly elaborate and some modest, but all peculiarly Laotian.

In religion as in almost everything else, the Laotians have worked out an adaptation that suits their own particular personality. One of their more charming fantasies, for instance, is the *Pagode des Hollandais,* as the French call it, or *Vat Pa Khe* in Laotian. About the middle of the seventeenth century some Dutch sailors and traders penetrated to the Laotian capital and so entertained the Laotians with their extraordinary habits and bizarre clothes that, later, when the pagoda was built, the craftsmen who carved the wooden doors leading to the shrine used the Dutchmen as a decorative motif. Traditionally the outer doors are carved with figures of gods and heroes who are supposed to frighten and confuse any evil spirits so that they cannot enter the shrine. In the *Pagode des Hollandais,* however, instead of the more familiar figures of dancing gods or fighting heroes from old legends, there are two worried-looking Dutchmen with tall hats and leggings, each with an enormous pipe in his hand. Because one Dutchman had arrived with a pet parrot, the bird had to be represented, too, but for the sake of symmetry those ancient craftsmen provided the strangers with two parrots each, one on each shoulder.

One of the most elaborate and sacred temples is the royal pagoda, Vat Mai, next to the king's palace and until recently the home of the gold image of Buddha, Prabang. Here the big lacquered pillars at the temple's entrance are covered with delicate designs of gold leaf. The high-pitched roof is beautifully constructed in a series of widening layers, each fronton an enormous triangle of carved and gilded wood, and the eaves support the characteristic rearing snakes, flying outward in golden ribbons in the clear mountain sunlight. Inside, too, the structure of the roof has a beautiful design of close-packed bamboo, rising in graded steps into the high darkness of the temple peak.

In other Buddhist countries the inside walls of such a shrine are often painted with scenes from the life of Buddha. The Laotians are apparently tired of this device and prefer to paint pictures that suit the mood of the particular artists assigned to the job. In Vat Mai there is a vigorous scene of dangerous fishing: enormous fish, with teeth bared, leap out of the water and fishermen who have fallen overboard try to scramble back into their boats.

The outer walls of a pagoda are often painted with scenes from the *Ramayana*, for much of the mythology of Southeast Asia still depends heavily on the influence that India wielded centuries ago. But in Laos, predictably enough, the ancient Hindu epic has been startlingly changed. The familiar story of the brave King Rama living disinherited in the forest with his beautiful Queen Sita starts out in the usual way. The drastic changes come when the wicked king of Lanka carries Sita off to his palace, for the Laotians find King Rama a tedious hero, preachy and solemn, while they prefer the king of Lanka for his commendable enterprise. According to the Laotians, Sita prefers the manly king of Lanka to a husband who is something of a stick. She is pleased when she is abducted, and peeved but resigned when Rama, with the help of Hanuman's army of monkeys, wins her back. They haven't actually changed the ending but obviously it seems to them unjust. They extend the story of the classic battle as long as they can and only at the very end, and with no sense of triumph, do they bring it to its traditional conclusion.

If the Laotians have taken liberties with the Hindu origins of their mythology, they have equally adapted Buddhism to suit their religious needs. In any pagoda the atmosphere is very casual. In the outer courtyard, or even on the steps of the shrine itself, children are playing or chickens strutting about. Nearby priests may be washing their saffron robes and hanging them up to dry. Women pause in the shade of a pagoda to exchange news, and small boys frequently stretch out to sleep on the cool floors of the entrance. Usually within the pagoda compound there is another house set a short distance apart, built on stilts like a typical Laotian house, with straw walls and a thatched roof. Inside, there will be food set out—rice, vegetables and chilis—and cooking utensils near a charcoal fire. This house is for the spirits of the earth and the air, and this remnant of an ancient animism is tended by the Buddhist priests attached to the pagoda.

In one way and another the Laotians have adapted both the temples and their religion to suit themselves, and thus it seems to them quite natural that all their festivals should be connected in some way with the pagodas in which they feel so cozy. All through Luang Prabang's dry season, in the wonderfully cool mountain nights, there are festivals almost every week. The Laotians have a genuine talent for fetes and can make a celebration out of almost anything. When, for instance, the defense minister was assassinated, the country went into mourning for a week. It started with the funeral and gradually turned into a festival with the last days of the week devoted to gambling, entertainment and drinking.

A marriage is celebrated with particular joy in Laos because it culminates something Laotians pursue with a great sense of what is correct and poetic—the art of courtship. In the evenings a young man of fourteen or fifteen will stand at the window of his chosen girl, or speak to her through a lattice or a bamboo hedge. He will say something like this: "Tonight the moon will be high and brilliant, but you are more beautiful than the moon.

You are as graceful as a bamboo in the wind, as tempting as a ripe papaya. No midnight is darker than your hair. But I am as ugly as a pig in the mud. . . ."

His girl will quickly reply, "No, no—you are blinded by your modesty. You are fleet as the deer in the forest, as skillful as the tiger in hunting . . . while I, I am so plain I dare not raise my head . . ." In wealthier circles and in the sophistication of the towns, however, marriages are more often arranged by the parents, but in any case, the ceremony itself means a celebration for friends and neighbors.

At such festivals, besides the usual entertainments and feasting, Laotian girls perform the dances which, like weaving, are part of a proper education. As in most of Southeast Asia the formal Laotian dances have their distant origins in India. But in Laos, the hand gestures have become wonderfully graceful with only the most fugitive resemblance to a more austere art. The basic themes are those activities in which a girl is most enticing—dressing her hair, threading flowers to make a garland or strolling through a garden.

Charming as the dances are, it is the professional storyteller who can hold the attention of a Laotian audience for hours on end—often all night. Indeed, sometimes the stories last eight days, which is not too surprising when you learn that many of them start with the beginning of the world—when earth and sky were linked by a giant liana, and people could climb up and down—and continue to the present day. After such extended listening, it is equally understandable that between one festival and the next Laotians have to spend a lot of time resting.

If you have been in Laos long enough to share a festival, to spend some time in Luang Prabang, to sit in a pagoda and exchange remarks with whoever comes by, to listen to a storyteller in a village, you will need no further justification of the Laotian way of life. Like them you will come to accept the idea that nothing matters much. It is enough to plant the rice and watch it grow; or weave your cloth and enjoy wearing it; or go to the temple and pray, or talk to your friends, or help prepare a festival; or to sit and think; or simply to sit and watch the village world go by. If all this seems an exasperating attitude for a nation that shares its borders with two Communist regions, that has seen repeated infringements of its frontiers, that has been defeated and annexed in countless wars, it is something that disturbs only the foreigners. If you ask a Laotian why his country doesn't take a more definite place in the tense issues of modern Indo-China, he is likely to reply gently with an old Laotian proverb that is an entirely satisfactory explanation to him, "The water drops, the ants eat the fish. The water rises, the fish eat the ants. So it is better to love than to hate."

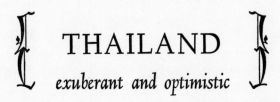

THAILAND

exuberant and optimistic

THE FIRST TIME THAT I EVER VISITED THAILAND, I arrived by land from Cambodia. This had involved a bus trip from Siemreap to the border (no railway there), and the day-long train ride from the border town of Aran Paknam to Bangkok. The immediate and (in Southeast Asia) startling thing that I had noticed in Thailand was that all the signs—the name of the railway station, the direction to the ticket office, the instructions about customs, hotel reservations and so on—were in Thai or Siamese. It was the first, and at that time the only, country in Southeast Asia that was not used to making concessions to at least one European language. Nothing else, I think, could have given me a more vivid clue to Thailand's recent history. Much of the present nature of the Thais, much of their enviable position in Southeast Asia, much of their relations with foreign powers are explained by the detail that struck me at the station—Thailand was never colonized by any European nation.

Riding on that train from the border to Bangkok, staring out of the window at the vast, seemingly inexhaustible rice fields of southern Thailand, the other major factor of Thai life was unintentionally impressed on me: Thailand is very rich. And, equally important, its wealth has largely stayed within the country because for most of the period that the rest of Southeast Asia was under Western rule, which skimmed off a large per-

111

centage of the natural wealth of the area, Thailand has managed to remain an independent nation.

This remarkable good fortune may not be immediately apparent when you first arrive in Bangkok. Like all Southeast Asian cities, it has its quota of noisy, overcrowded bazaars, of dirty roads and unpaved alleys between tenements, of densely filled and grasping Chinese sections engaged in minor trading and business activity. Its main street is a narrow bedlam of shops, stalls, shady-looking money-changers and imposing bank or insurance buildings. It is jammed with cars, taxis, pedicabs, rickshaws. But even in the least distinctive sections of Bangkok you will notice a difference of atmosphere, a freer manner, a more casual acceptance of the foreigner, combined with a self-contained confidence in the Thai way of living and doing things.

Of course, in its long history, Thailand has not always maintained its national integrity with such unruffled certainty. Chinese records show that in 2000 B.C. the people of what is now Thailand had traveled as far as China to conquer part of the Yangtze Valley and set up their own princely kingdom. Centuries later, on the great wave of Indian expansion, Indian immigrants came to Thailand with their own peculiar brand of cultural and religious subjugation. Later still, part of Thailand was absorbed by the flourishing Khmer dynasty of Cambodia, part of it was conquered by the Burmese, and the long arm of Thailand that extends down the Malay peninsula became a province of the great Sri Vijayan empire with its capital in Palembang on the Indonesian island of Sumatra.

Eventually the princes and leaders of Thailand began to assert themselves against this foreign partition and domination of their country. In the north the prince Mengrai led a successful revolution against the Burmese near the end of the thirteenth century and founded the first formal Thai capital in Chiengmai. There have been many shifts and changes of capital since then, but even today people in Thailand are apt to insist that Chiengmai is the most beautiful, the most truly "Thai" of their cities. It is saturated with Thai history and feeling in a way that even the greatest of the later Thai capitals are not. When you visit it now, you find a quiet, provincial, northern town, by-passed by history and the exigencies of commerce and international exchange, gently decaying, but always with a singular character and appeal. Its mood is so strong that it produces some rather unusual effects on people. For instance, one well-known gentleman who lives in Chiengmai and likes to give large parties insists that all his guests come dressed in the ancient Thai manner—calf-length draped trousers with a short, loose jacket fastening only at the neck for the men, and pleated sarongs in heavy silk with a tight bodice for the women. If by some chance a guest does not possess this costume or forgets to wear it, he will courteously be led away by a servant to a dressing room, will be provided with suitable clothes to wear, and only then will he be permitted to join the other guests and share in the traditional Thai food and entertainment that his host offers. The special Chiengmai dish which is served on all such festive occasions is *mu som*—barbecued suckling pig stuffed with oranges and vegetables.

It is the second largest city in Thailand, but its atmosphere is entirely different from the modern bustle of Bangkok, and, in fact, the people of Chiengmai view the present capital and its life with a good deal of scorn. They find Bangkok *nouveau riche*, flashy and pleasure-loving, and attribute these traits to the fact that the south is too rich for its own good. Of course, Chiengmai is pretty rich too—it is situated on a fertile plain, surrounded on two sides by high mountains, irrigated by the Me Ping, a northern branch of the Chao Phya River. It has extensive rice cultivation, tobacco and teak and is famous for its handicrafts, particularly silver, pottery and silk. Chiengmai is particularly proud of its silks, which are heavy and lustrous and which (according to Chiengmai taste) are far more subtle in color and design than the bright and vulgarly arresting silks of the south.

Bangkok, in return, has its own sly comments to make about Chiengmai. Because of its proximity to the Shan States of Burma where opium is grown fairly freely, Chiengmai is supposed to be an important center of opium smuggling. When one Bangkok businessman asks another what sort of trade he is engaged in or what its location is, if the reply is, "I have a business in Chiengmai," this is immediately a signal for shouts of knowing laughter, for in business circles this remark is taken to refer only to some illegal transaction.

However, many of the people of Bangkok still love to go to Chiengmai, considering it a pleasant holiday resort. It is only a few hours away by air, and, compared with the steamy monotony of the climate in the capital, Chiengmai is cool in the summer and in winter becomes cold enough for fires in the evenings and sweaters or coats in the day. This seems to be a particularly good climate for flowers all the year round, and Chiengmai roses are known throughout the kingdom for their perfection and their scent.

Because of a strong tradition of matriarchy, Chiengmai women are supposed to be more resourceful and independent than southerners. They have much more freedom, socially and economically, and polyandry is not unusual among them. This, inevitably, has led to a familiar joke in Bangkok: with a slightly dashing inflection a man may say, "I like to spend my vacations

114

in Chiengmai. The climate is so good and the Chiengmai roses are so beautiful and generous." Everyone knows that he is off for an illicit weekend. A Thai friend of mine told me that if I ever heard a husband remark (even with a serious or dedicated expression), "I will renounce the sensuous pleasure of Bangkok and seek salvation in Chiengmai," it meant only that he was bored with marital life and was looking for other distractions. This particular reason for a visit to Chiengmai is made even more attractive by the fact that Chiengmai women are extremely handsome and very clothes conscious—the legend is that they will starve to death in order to dress well.

There are, however, more conventional and respectable reasons for going to Chiengmai. Even though, during the wars between the Thais, the Cambodians and the Burmese, the city lay directly on the invasion route and was destroyed and plundered many times, still enough of its historic architecture remains to give an indication of past glories. Chiengmai architecture is quite distinctive in style and is considered by the Thais much more elegant than that of Bangkok. They feel that it expresses the restrained chic of the Chiengmai temperament, while the Bangkok temples, which are later in date, reflect the south's inclination toward the grandiose and gaudy.

In a way the most illuminating of the Chiengmai temples is the Wat Phra Singh, the Temple of the Lion. It is not the earliest, nor is it the best known, but it is well preserved and has the rather curious distinction of representing many of the different historic styles of northern architecture. Each style is shown in a separate building, and altogether the temple compound becomes a kind of compact, visual history book. The Thais, for the most part, prefer the Temple of the Royal Pagoda (Wat Chedi Luang), which is older and is still considered the most important in Chiengmai and one of the most grand and imposing in Thailand. Older still, and strongly reminiscent of Cambodian architecture, is the Temple of the Seven-tiered Pagoda (Phra Chedi Wat Ched Yod), and there, more clearly than anywhere else in Chiengmai, are the reminders in style and decoration of Thailand's ancient connections with Indian and Hindu culture.

Although so much deep Thai sentiment is connected with Chiengmai, its founder is not so greatly celebrated in Thai history as his friend and fellow liberator Phra Ruang, an almost legendary hero who started his career as a water carrier in the personal service of the Khmer king and ended by freeing his people from Khmer rule. He established a new capital (Sukhothai), where he was crowned king; he initiated a new Thai royal dynasty, ruled and fought brilliantly, stretched the Thai frontiers to approximately their present scope and built enormous pagodas to show his Buddhist devotion.

However, the grandeur and eminence of Sukhothai lasted only one century, and then the dynasty changed and so did the capital, this time to the extraordinary city of Ayudhya, which came to be known as "The Incomparable." For over four hundred years Ayudhya grew and prospered; its splendid temples and towering gilded images of Buddha became famous all over Asia, until the Burmese invaded Thailand and besieged the city. After a year of attrition Ayudhya fell. The Burmese sacked the city, destroyed the temples and images and left the magnificent palaces and monuments in ruins.

If you have a taste for the melancholy fascinations of deserted cities, it is worth making the two-hour train trip from Bangkok to Ayudhya. There, in its odd and pleasant setting—scattered over a number of islands in the Menam—is the old capital with more than a hundred ruined temples still remaining from the many

116

hundreds that must at one time have been there. Of these the best-known and principal one is the Wat Phra Srisanbej, a tall slender spire, carved in circular ridges like a spring, set on top of a stupa which, in turn, is reached by steep, disintegrating stairs.

The most impressive of the remaining monuments is an immense bronze statue of Buddha—the largest of its sort in the world—which must at one time have been surrounded by a proportionately imposing temple. Now the protecting walls have all crumbled away except for the cracked, precarious wall in front of the image, and all that remains of the halls and corridors of five or six hundred years ago are a few carved steps and platforms, the slender elegance of a few pillars, and, of course, the massive, contemplative figure of the Buddha set, now, in full sunlight against the sky.

You can, if you wish, return to Bangkok by river launch (stopping to visit the royal summer palace of Bang Pa In on the way), and can see on the banks of the wide, slow-moving river the gently-paced life of the villages. Many of the wooden houses with their peaked roofs—usually dominated by the spire of glistening tiles of a temple—are built out over the river. Narrow boats, paddled by men or women in wide straw hats, skim about between the houses and the villages. For longer trips larger boats with square sails and a flapping awning rigged to protect the passengers carry the traffic on the river. And always, beyond the villages, beyond the river life, the *va et vien* of buying, selling, visiting, stretch the rice fields, the vast, rich, flat southern plain of Thailand that produces its wealth and determines its life.

During the great days of Ayudhya—Thailand's Golden Age —the city that is now Bangkok was nothing more than a cluster of fishing huts on the swampy banks of the Menam River near the delta. Near the end of the eighteenth century, however, after new kings and liberators had re-established Thai independence, Bangkok became the capital and Thailand entered its subtle, complex, shrewdly maneuvered relations with the West. Up to that moment, except for some instruction in the use of Western firearms that some Portuguese had left with the Thais, and the contributions of a few French doctors, which had included some medicines and, mysteriously, a recipe for sponge cake, Thailand had virtually no diplomatic or commercial contact with the West. But during the nineteenth century the Thais proved themselves to be remarkably adept at using the British (who were in Malaya) to help them secure their shifting western frontier in return for help in subduing the Burmese (who were, in any case, the traditional Thai enemies). With the same mixture of canniness and self-protection they used the French in Indo-China to secure their eastern boundaries. They then played the French and the British off against each other to maintain their national independence—and managed it all with that peculiarly autocratic, offhand manner combined with a sharp sense of a bargain that seems to have been a characteristic of Thai kings. Years later, when American influence was growing in Asia, the Thais managed to play both the French and the British off against the Americans to secure commercial advantages, aid and protection from all three.

In modern Bangkok you can find strains of all the various institutions and traditions and types of people that have between them built and run the city. Thailand is still a monarchy even though its monarch is no longer an absolute ruler. Reformer kings brought in some democratic measures; military *coups d'état* further curtailed royal power. The government, however, still remains pretty autocratic, and based on military control. The people don't seem to mind, and foreign powers that make a great fuss about "nondemocratic" nations in other parts of Asia seem to have no trouble in coming to terms with the Thais. The tourist, at least, can be grateful for the continuation of royal traditions and institutions in Thailand, for they are responsible for some of the prettiest and most distinctive aspects of the capital.

The Grand Palace, a miniature walled town within the city, is set on the bank of the river and could well be an illustration from some book of exotic fairytales. Your Thai friends will tell you that the best moment to see it is at sunset from a boat on the river. Certainly, for that short span of time every clear evening, it has the unreal spell of a musical-comedy set. The crenellated, white walls turn ice-cream pink. Above them the yellow tiles of the high-pitched roofs shine golden in the slanting light, the thin gilded snakes on the eaves make ribbons of light in the sky, the towers and spires of the temples glitter with the improbably brilliant flashing lights of diamonds, emeralds, rubies. Of course, when you visit the Grand Palace the next morning you realize that the golden sunset moment was romanticizing only paint or the high glaze of pottery, that the jewel-encrusted towers are set only with bits of colored glass or mirrors, that the charming pink walls are only whitewash over plaster. But even so, that moment's illusion is part of the glamour that surrounds Thai royalty.

Within the enclosed area of the Grand Palace you will find the most famous building in Thailand, Wat Phra Keo or the Temple of the Emerald Buddha. There, in an open courtyard, stand the half-dozen buildings and shrines that make up the temple area. Around the whole group are protective galleries, walled on the outside, open on the inside, exuberantly painted with murals of scenes and stories from the *Ramayana* epic, guarded at the entrances by enormous statues, covered with gleaming tiles, of giants and demons. Beyond the galleries is another protective wall around the temple itself, guarded this time by bronze lions, and then, rising elegantly above it, there are the inlaid pillars, the elaborately decorated walls, the soaring roofs of Wat Phra Keo. As you walk through the deep porticoes, cross the brass thresholds between massive carved doors, you are followed always by the frivolous tinkling of hundreds of tiny wind bells hanging from the eaves.

All this decoration, protection, art, imagination and reverence is directed toward an image that may seem to you unimpressive when you first see it. Deep in the innermost shrine, enthroned on top of a fabulously ornate gilt altar, seated under a golden canopy, surrounded by gold and silver miniature trees and an astonishing array of treasures, sheltered by a red-and-gold roof and walls painted with sacred scenes from the life of Buddha, is a small, greenish figure of Buddha, made of jasper (not emerald). This image, however, contains for Thailand and for a large part of Southeast Asia such intense historical and religious significance that even now there is a bitter controversy between Laos and Thailand about its proper home and treatment. The legend is that it was made by the king of the gods for a devout religious teacher in India. From him it traveled to Ceylon and later to various capitals in Thailand, later still to the Laotian royal city of Luang Prabang and eventually to Bangkok, where it now has a particular identification with the protection and divine right of Thai royalty.

All around the enclosure of the Temple of the Emerald Buddha, within the Grand Palace walls, are hundreds more buildings and monuments—shrines, palaces, libraries, ministries, stupas, a pavilion where the king receives his ceremonial bath, a gilt throne for royal audiences, a procession-watching pavilion built on top of the palace wall, a hall for statues of ancestors, a shrine for the cremation ashes of former kings. Altogether it is one of the most extraordinary and extravagant groups of buildings in Southeast Asia. Of course, there are many more temples, famous statues of Buddha and royal possessions scattered through Bangkok, but none of them, I think, have the scale, charm or interest of the Grand Palace.

Another royal prerogative that the Thai kings, like their Cambodian counterparts, maintain, is the tradition of palace dancers. Here too, on ceremonial occasions when they perform in the royal parks, the general public can have a chance to see the wonderfully expert ballets, the gorgeous costumes, the magnificent scenes of gods and demons from the old epics. Many of the Thai nobility still keep up their old tradition of aristocracy by studying classical dancing themselves, and even if the present young king is better known in the rest of the world for his love of American jazz, still on formal occasions he appears before his people to watch the dances that his family have protected for generations.

Alongside this great royal heritage in Bangkok is the brisk modern life of a rapidly spreading Western influence. For some years before the war it was fashionable for those families that could afford it to send their sons to be educated in England. (A rather irreverent Thai friend of mine calls them "the old school Thais.") They returned to Bangkok bringing with them a taste for the life of English-style clubs and Western entertainment—parties, dances, Western sports. Much of this influence spread, and when you first arrive in Bangkok you can't help noticing that here, more than in any other city of Southeast Asia, people wear Western clothes. As you stay longer, you find that

121

Thais invite you to their houses more readily than other Southeast Asians, but are equally at ease in a life of restaurants, movies, spectator sports. They move between their two worlds with no apparent strain—often at a party your Thai friends will politely speak to you in English, but if they get interested in an argument, or have a joke to tell, they will break into their own language (which lends itself particularly well to puns and plays on words) for the greater enjoyment of their fellow countrymen. They may happily go with you to a night club modeled on a French pattern and be perfectly at home, but equally they will dance the *lamtong* in the Thai or Chinese dance halls.

They watch with the absorbed attention of a connoisseur the popular Bangkok entertainment of "Siamese boxing"—an alarming display of kicks, leaps, punches and lethal expert blows with the side of the hand—all accompanied by a peculiarly Siamese combination of dance, religious ceremony and prayer. They attend, with a comparably knowing criticalness, say, a tennis match. In the very well-attended Silpakorn Theatre they produce, with their own adaptation of Western technique and Thai content, charming plays written and acted in the language of the country, but employing all the devices of Western staging. One play, for instance, that I saw there concerned a sea nymph, and with an entirely Western sense of realism the underwater scenes were staged with gauze curtains and hidden platforms to produce the startlingly accurate effect of an aquarium.

My own preference is for *likay*, the rapid, ribald, "popular" theatre of Bangkok. The surroundings, naturally, are nowhere near as fancy as the theatres or formal outdoor stages where the classical dances or the plays approved by the Department of Fine Arts appear. Of the ten or fifteen *likay* theatres in the city, most of them are flimsy wooden structures—easily collapsed, often moved—in the bazaar or less Western sections of town. You crowd in with the cheerful, chattering crowd to find a place on one of the wooden benches that face the simplest of wooden stages and a sagging, patched curtain. Sometimes, for the festivals that seem to happen just about every month at one temple or another, the *likay* stage is set up in the temple courtyard and concentrates a large part of the gaiety of the occasion.

The plays themselves are, in their peculiarly insouciant way, historical and deal mostly with the long series of wars between Burma and Thailand. Out of those centuries of rather disorganized fighting came countless stories of heroes, victories, defeats, stratagems and tricks; these are enacted in the plays with many delicious (but expected) surprises. The farmer's daughter with whom the young prince falls in love turns out to be a princess in disguise. The unknown soldier who performs a heroic act and changes the course of the battle is discovered to be, after all, the rightful heir to the throne. There are kings and queens, intrigues and fighting in every play. The dialogues are half sung, and sometimes there are brief dances.

Recently, since the visit of Burma's Prime Minister, U Nu, to Thailand and the occasion of his journey to the ancient capital of Ayudhya to plant some sacred Buddhist trees as an act of penance for the Burmese destruction of the city two hundred years ago, the content of many of the *likay* plays has changed to a gentler interpretation of Thailand's traditional enemy. However, it isn't really the historical aspects of the plays that continue to draw the Thai audiences in such large numbers. If you are sensible you will go to any *likay* play with someone who can interpret for you because the joy of the performance is, to a great extent, in the improvisations of the actors on the stage— different with every performance. They are judged by their skill in keeping to the poetic form that *likay* dialogue demands (comparable to passages of heroic couplets in the Western world), but they insert, in the course of the play, their own additions, comments, jokes, satiric remarks on current affairs, politics, personalities or any other subject of topical interest. Then you can, with at least some understanding, join in the explosions of laughter or loud yells of disapproval that the un-inhibited audience makes a part of the *likay* performance.

This marvelously exuberant, rather impious sense of fun is, to me, the most attractive quality about Bangkok. There are no hangovers of colonial bitterness, no insecurities about Thai cul-ture, habits or preferences, no nervous uncertainties and sus-picions of Western influences. All around you there will be the growing imprints of the most recent foreign influx into Thailand—American cars on the roads, American goods in the shops, American buildings, factories, businesses going up, a lavish new international airport—but this deep characteristic of an independent, self-confident, optimistic approach to life re-mains the most noticeable aspect of Bangkok. While the shiny new cars or buildings move into the city, still, along the many canals and waterways in and around Bangkok, the floating markets continue to flourish, housewives in search of flowers, vegetables, fish, continue to take a narrow boat down to their favorite vendors to shop for what they want with their traditional sharp-eyed discrimination. The temples and their festivals are still a basic part of Thai life. If foreigners like the speed and comfort of taxis, many Thais prefer the exchange of gossip or a joke or a quick, skeptical remark with the pedicab driver and the slower view of their wide, confusing, many-faceted city that the pedicab ride gives them.

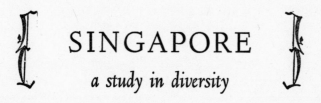

SINGAPORE

a study in diversity

IF YOU STAND ON ANY BUSY STREET CORNER IN
Singapore at, say, five o'clock of any working day, you will see
one of the world's most remarkably cosmopolitan processions of
people streaming out of shops and office buildings, waiting for
buses, pushing their way onto streetcars, hurrying to appoint-
ments in one of the big downtown hotels. A large proportion of
the crowd will be Chinese, old men walking slowly, wearing
the traditional long robe and soft shoes of an era that has vanished
in their homeland, or young students in Western clothes, their
hair slicked back with brilliantine, and inevitably, among them,
the type of student that is a familiar sight in any university
town, with unkempt hair, eccentric clothes, heavy-rimmed glasses,
in earnest discussion of Jean-Paul Sartre or politics. Some of
the Chinese women will be old-fashioned, their long hair
knotted high on the back of their head; some will still wear the
blue cotton tunic and trousers of a China they have almost
forgotten; some will wear the newest styles from Hong Kong,
the sleek, tight sheath dresses slashed high to the thigh; they
will have adopted the Audrey Hepburn haircut or the elaborate
curls of a permanent; they will pause before the advertisements
for a movie that may be American, Indian, Chinese, Japanese,
English or French; they will chatter like sparrows among themselves, pretending not to notice the young men eying them as
they pass.

127

Mixed in among the Chinese faces of the crowd, you will see samples of all the other elements of Singapore's population. The policeman on the street corner may well be a bearded and turbaned Sikh from north India. The man who owns the shoeshop behind you may be a south or west Indian and may be dressed in Western clothes or in the Indian achkan or dhoti. The women will be in saris or the tunics, veils and loose trousers of north India. The assistant in the airlines office across the street might be American, English or Australian and will probably wear the usual tropical outfit of white drill trousers and open shirt. Now and again you will catch sight of an Indonesian sarong, or a Muslim fez, or the uniforms of sailors from a dozen different countries. Certainly you will see Eurasians of every variety, but strangely rare and difficult to spot will be the members of the Malay community—the original inhabitants of Singapore.

The reasons for both the diversity of Singapore's population and for the scarcity of Malays is easy enough to guess. By now the city is well known as a center of commerce and shipping, the ideal crossroads and market place for travel and trade in Asia. When you walk through the shopping districts and see the stores (unlike those in the rest of Southeast Asia) filled with merchandise from all over the world, you will remember that Singapore is largely a free port. You will notice that prices are, on the whole, reasonable, that there are relatively few taxes, that half a dozen different currencies are acceptable and can be changed into Malaya's own Straits dollars—again, a rarity in Asia. Naturally these easy conditions and busy commercial life of Singapore have attracted traders, merchants and businessmen from all over Asia and from Europe as well. In their wake came their families and a steady flow of doctors, lawyers, teachers, entertainers, representing all the needs and amusements of a community. Meanwhile, the Malays, who have never been renowned as businessmen, who have always been less aggressive than their neighbors, retreated more and more to the inland, lived in the upcountry towns and villages, farming or working in Malaya's vast rubber plantations. Singapore had in less than a hundred years become an altogether hostile environment for them.

Singapore, which was eventually to become associated in people's minds with so many clichés of colonialism—"the White Man's Burden," "an Outpost of Empire"—which gave, with its establishment, a literal truth to "the sun never sets on the British Empire," was founded in 1819 by one of England's most dramatic and adventurous empire builders. Thomas Stamford Bingley Raffles began his career at fourteen as a clerk in the East India Company, earning a guinea a month. In 1805, at the age of twenty-three, accompanied by a new bride, he set out on the long sea voyage by one of the sailing ships called East Indiamen to his first post in Asia, a minor government appointment in Penang on the Malayan coast. From that moment until his death in 1826, his career, his work, his interest, his affection and his life were taken up by Southeast Asia. He was involved in many astonishing incidents of British history. He was, for instance, largely responsible for England's brief capture of Java; he explored the jungles of Sumatra and was appointed resident at Bencoolen there; he was agent to the governor general of Malacca; he wrote a history of Java; he represented the government in Samarang; he halted the slave trade. He was knighted by Queen Victoria and eventually he was indicted by Parliament and returned to England in disgrace. After all the glory and all the scandals, he was at last acquitted of the charges against him just before his sudden death at the age of forty-five. But, after all the ups and downs of his career, Raffles will be best remembered for the unscrupulous, unauthorized, unsupported act which got him into so much trouble at home, and turned out to be one of the most valuable services that any Englishman had rendered his country in the nineteenth century—the founding of Singapore.

The site of the port city became a part of the British Empire in an almost classically picturesque way—with the planting of the Union Jack on the Singapore beach. Behind that action, predictably enough, were the usual negotiations with local rulers, the exploitation of local grievances, the appearance of six British ships in the harbor, the tacit display of power, the arrangement with the Sultan of the area (according to Emily Hahn's delightful biography of Raffles, he paid the Sultan "a thousand dollars, a roll of black broadcloth, a roll of yellow broadcloth, and a fixed allowance agreed on between them"). With a characteristic combination, then, of diplomacy, bribery and the possibility of force, another British colony was established. Even today you can scarcely move in Singapore without being reminded of the vital part Raffles played in its founding. Apart from the famous Raffles Hotel, there are the Raffles College, Raffles Library, Raffles Museum, and of course a memorial statue of him; there is a Raffles Place, a Raffles Quay, and dozens of other casual or deliberate references to his place in Singapore's history.

Immediately, even before the city was built, its commercial potential was recognized. According to a local, contemporary commentator, traders and merchandise flooded into the Lion City (*singha*—lion; *pura*—town or temple). Miss Hahn records that "Every day auctions were being held, four or five at a time in different parts of the new town. All the houses were hastily built ones of atap, for there was no time to build brick ones." A year after its founding, Raffles himself wrote of Singapore, "Its trade already far exceeds what Malacca could boast of during the most flourishing years." Very soon merchant ships from all over Europe and Asia crowded Singapore's excellent harbor. In nearly a century and a half since, the essential character of Singapore hasn't changed. It acquired an added importance when the British developed it into their biggest foreign naval base, but at heart Singapore remains a new, sprawling, shrewd, money-minded, international city, with overtones of a distant dream of empire.

To many people modern life in Singapore carries faintly ridiculous overtones. It is lightly reminiscent of old Noel Coward songs about the Englishman in Asia, of the social life of old-fashioned empire builders in the Singapore Club or Raffles Hotel, of foggy discussions about the "natives" conducted in an atmosphere of gin slings, gin fizzes or planter's punch. Of course, this particular fantasy of Singapore life was given a grim reality during the war. The Englishmen were indeed sipping their tea or their drinks in clubs and bars, gazing complacently out to their "impregnable" naval base, which they often called the Gibraltar of the Orient, when the Japanese armies, experienced in jungle fighting, quietly captured Singapore from the land three months after the Pacific war began. They crossed the great causeway that links the island of Singapore with the state of Johore and the inland jungles and plantations of Malaya, attacking from the one direction that the British had thought impossible and had never bothered to protect. Singapore fell in a few hours and the British were compelled to flee in whatever order they could manage, abandoning vast quantities of troops and equipment.

After the Japanese occupation and the return of the British following the war, life in Singapore was never the same again. There was the constant push from the city's polyglot population for the end of British rule. This resistance flared into open rebellion in upcountry Malaya—a situation that was difficult to cure or to come to terms with since it was strongly championed and assisted by Communist elements. Enlightened governors, new and more liberal policies in Singapore itself showed the British willingness to follow in Malaya the same program of non-acrimonious withdrawal that they had used in their other Asian colonies. However, the continuous state of revolution, the increasing power of the Communists, and the difficulties of forming an independent Malay government in a country where the major population was Chinese, the commercial and political power was in the hands of the British, the Chinese and the Indians, and where the Malays themselves were the least influential group made a reasonable settlement hopeless for the present.

Altogether these conditions have presented a puzzling and so far insoluble problem. Because of the troubles, it is virtually impossible or at least very difficult to travel in the interior of Malaya. You can visit (by air) some of the coastal towns like Penang or planters' strongholds like Kuala Lumpur, which are scenically lovely and give you a brief glimpse of an earlier life of pleasant weekends at the beach and the quiet routine of a provincial town. But nowadays they are so hedged around by restrictions, have such a jumpy, uneasy atmosphere, that they are scarcely the places to choose for a holiday visit.

In Singapore itself, there are still reminders of the prewar days in the British life of the city. The big Western-style hotels like the Raffles, the Cockpit or Seaview are still filled for the most part with European visitors or residents; the bars and cocktail lounges are still patronized by Englishmen in tropical whites having a "sundowner"; the clubs, the weekend sports of sailing, cricket, golf, still continue with an almost exclusively Western clientele. On the fashionable "dance nights" at the hotels, although you will see a few saris or Chinese gowns, for the most part the dancers and drinkers will be in pale summer evening dresses and white dinner jackets. Occasionally entertainers from Europe will arrive for a short tour (when I was there Dame Sybil Thorndike and her husband Sir Lewis Casson gave a series of recitations in the Singapore Victoria Memorial Hall); sometimes a pianist or a violinist will arrive for a couple of recitals, accompanied by the Singapore orchestra, and on those occasions Singapore society turns out with great formality to hear these echoes from home.

To me, the more colorful and more lively life in Singapore is found in the Chinese sections of the city. There you can sample the wonderful food in the restaurants, shop around for the silks, brocades, linen and lace from China, or spend hours in antique shops surrounded by porcelain, ivory, jade and lacquer. These are only a few more obvious aspects of the full, entirely Chinese city life which flourishes within the city life of Singapore.

The Chinese in Singapore have, for instance, the largest Chinese university outside Peking—a university with enough status and importance to persuade the celebrated Dr. Lin Yutang to move to Singapore and become its president. (He has since resigned on issues of internal politics.) Besides the commercial and political power the Chinese wield as a community, they have their prominent individuals in every field. The mayor of Singapore is Chinese; in every major body of local administration, the Chinese are represented. The Chinese have produced their millionaires, their eccentrics, their writers, their artists. Perhaps the most unusual of all these was the man known as the Tiger Balm King because he made his first fortune by selling in fabulous amounts a kind of patented ointment called Tiger Balm. He later made new fortunes in newspapers and other business ventures. His empire spread to include both Singapore and Hong Kong, and his amazing houses and gardens are a legend in both cities.

One of the most odd and amusing sights in Singapore is the garden he built for the enjoyment of the public. There, with a ticket that costs a few cents, you can walk through the Chinese archway into a child's wild fantasy. Among the lawns and flowerbeds are scattered large plaster models of dragons, snakes, werewolves, alternated, rather surprisingly, with timid nursery-story animals like rabbits, ducks and piglets. In one section of the park there are plaster statues and tableaux illustrating famous Chinese murders, all painted with gruesome fidelity to the gaudy color of clothes and the vivid streams of blood from wounds. There are also more joyful tableaux showing the Chinese New Year's festivities, or a favorite scene from a Chinese play, to change your mood continually as you walk through the park.

The Chinese seem to have a talent for this diverting kind of muddle. My favorite place of entertainment in Singapore was a large amusement park called "The Happy World." Again, you pay a few cents' entrance fee, and this time you find yourself in a bedlam of sound, activity and gaiety. Loud-speakers blare out Chinese songs and movie music, relieved occasionally with American jazz. All around you is a bustling, frivolous bazaar, with stalls where you can buy toys for the children, candy and cakes, genuine American blue jeans (very chic among the Singapore youth), umbrellas, embroidered Chinese slippers to wear around the house, nylon blouses (also very chic).

As you move further into The Happy World, you come to the stalls where you can have your fortune told, can gamble with cards, dice, numbers and something I didn't understand that involved sticks and blocks of wood. You can see peep shows, try your skill in shooting galleries, or simply admire a new motorcycle from England revolving alone in glistening splendor on a turntable. The children run screaming among the Ferris wheels, the merry-go-rounds, the miniature speedboats, the dodgem cars, the pinball machines in the penny arcade.

Conveniently placed among the amusements are restaurants and snack bars. One of the restaurants is discreetly elegant; you are served excellent (and expensive) food on a terrace, and as you sample the specialties of the house—Singapore's delicious shrimp, crayfish, sharks' fins, seaweed—you can look out across The Happy World as the short tropical evening deepens, watch the lights come on in the city and in the harbor, while below you the shops and stalls and entertainments come to a sudden glaring life of neon lights. There are other cheaper, rowdier restaurants where you sit on the sidewalk on wooden benches, sharing your table with whoever happens to sit down there, yell your order to the red-faced cook busy and precise in the back of the room, order the light golden Chinese wine served hot, and settle down to talk and joke with your neighbors. If you know enough about Chinese cooking you can also give the cook special instructions about your preferences—no coriander in the soup, or plenty of ginger in the sauce for the fish—you can dig your fingers into the enormous fish flopped out on a stone slab in front of the cooking bench to be sure it is fresh, or choose among the plucked fowl hanging from the ceiling the particular one that you want to eat. You are surrounded by a cheerful, friendly atmosphere and the exhilarating company of people out to enjoy themselves for the evening.

After dinner, if you have exhausted the other entertainments, you can visit one or all of the three theatres in The Happy World. One will be exhibiting a Chinese movie, another will probably have a modern Chinese play, and the third will certainly have some version of classical Peking opera. You can take your choice between the slow-moving cadences of the historical romances that seem to appeal most to film makers (no English subtitles) and the loud, clanging music that accompanies the opera, the penetrating nasal tones of the singers, the magnificent mixture of comedy, tragedy, history that makes up the plots. (One of the favorite sequences in Peking opera is a half-danced, half-acted incident that involves a widow on the way to her husband's grave who flirts outrageously with the official who accompanies her.) Or you can sample the soberer modern plays of social problems, economic difficulties, politics and divided loyalties.

Of course, each of the smaller communities of Singapore has its special life and activity in the city, too, on a more limited scale. The Indians with their own restaurants, their shops where you can buy saris and Indian sandals, their own temples, shrines and community life, are an essential part of Singapore. Any morning in the city's English-language newspaper, the *Straits Times,* you can read that, perhaps, a troupe of Indonesian dancers will be performing somewhere in Singapore, or you will see a picture story of the dances and celebrations that accompany a local festival in some upcountry village, or you will see the announcements of cricket matches, yacht races, a charity dance, a concert, an art exhibit of the European community. All of it is a part of the life of Singapore, and all of it contributes to the city's interracial, intercultural, multilingual—in short, cosmopolitan—atmosphere.

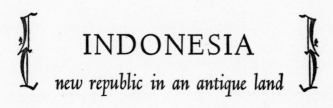

INDONESIA
new republic in an antique land

A YOUNG AMERICAN FRIEND OF MINE WHO HAS
lived and studied in Indonesia was asked by several universities
on his return home recently to give lectures about his Indonesian
experiences. In the discussion periods afterward, he told me,
the first question almost invariably asked was: "When will the
French quit?" or, "Do you think that the United States should
continue to give aid to the French?"

My friend patiently explained that the French were in *Indo-
China,* and that although the Dutch had ruled Indonesia for 350
years, the country had been free for the past six, and that America, far from aiding the Dutch, had come out strongly for Indonesia's independence. This explanation usually was greeted with
polite surprise by his audiences, and eventually he found it
expedient to begin all his speeches: "The last time I gave a talk
about Indonesia, the first question I was asked . . ."

This curious innocence abroad about Southeast Asia's largest
country (both in size and in population) is not entirely surprising even when world attention is so nervously focused there.
One's associations with the actual names of the Indonesian islands
are apt to be of distant adventurous days. Java or Sumatra recalls
the time early explorers found the fabulous Spice Islands, and
the wars for their possession by the European nations. In those
wild days astonishing private fortunes were made; pirates hunted
the priceless cargoes of nutmeg, pepper, cloves; and the food
habits of all Europe changed. A seasoning as ordinary (now)

as pepper was so rare, and obtained at such risk, that to this day there is a phrase in Dutch for anything outrageously expensive—"it's as costly as pepper."

Borneo calls up, in a way, even wilder pictures of deep and dangerous forests, treacherous mountains and Dyak head-hunters. Bali and Celebes suggest, perhaps, gentler, more lushly tropical landscapes. As for the Lesser Sunda Islands, fragments of land as small as Komodo or bigger islands like Flores, or the group of islands that surround Halmahera—an archipelago within an archipelago—well, most Westerners have never heard of them at all unless they were involved in the New Guinea campaign in World War II and the slow, difficult combination of jungle warfare and island hopping that followed.

Apart from these distant or painful associations modern Indonesia is, not without reason, the least-known country of Southeast Asia. For hundreds of years, under colonial rule, it maintained a strangely insulated life. While tourism was not exactly discouraged, Indonesia's few visitors nearly always went to the island of Bali—one of the few places in the country people outside have heard of. Trade, commerce and the natural wealth of the country were owned almost exclusively by the Dutch and the Chinese. Indonesians themselves were kept in startling ignorance of the rest of the world, with poor educational facilities and chances to travel. Six years ago when I was in Jogjakarta, an Indonesian remarked to me, "Until now, the easiest way for an Indonesian to travel was to offend the Dutch and get exiled to Holland." He was speaking from experience—as one of Indonesia's pioneer agitators for better education he had spent several years in exile for starting the first free Indonesian-language schools. On another occasion, in Japan, I met some Indonesian college students who had been allowed to enter Japanese universities—but then were not permitted to return home. Even now, it is hard to find books in English on the extraordinary history of Indonesia, on its literature, legends, or (always excepting Bali) its arts.

At least one good thing has come out of all this isolation: for the adventurous traveler Indonesia is the most exciting land in Southeast Asia. Its range is enormous. You can stay in the cultural capitals of Central Java in a civilization so rarefied that it is almost decadent, or you can explore islands that are literally uncharted and jungles that have never been penetrated. Everywhere, even the looks of the people are a record of their long, complex history. The basic Malay stock of brown-skinned people of medium height and build, with black hair and a fleeting reminder of their part-Mongol ancestry in the set of their eyes, is modified in dozens of ways in the various islands.

In Sumatra you will notice, especially along the coast, a more aquiline cast of feature, for the island has a long history of trade and religious association with the Middle East. The Javanese, lighter of skin, show traces of their Indian contacts. Bali, until very recently, was pretty much left alone, and the Balinese with their round faces and big gentle eyes are perhaps nearer the original Malay settlers. But then, again, in the more obscure regions there are pockets of civilizations left over from pre-Malay days—the Borneo Dyaks or the north Sumatran Bataks or the Melanesians of the easternmost islands. And in the cities there is the added complexity of enormous Chinese settlements and smaller Indian, Arab and Eurasian populations. In that long curving archipelago that links Malaya to Australia you can find some of the most beautiful islands in the world, arts of an excellence unmatched in Southeast Asia, and some of the most appealing people anywhere.

It is a pity that most visitors to Indonesia arrive in its capital, Jakarta, a depressingly ugly city sprawling about docks and canals and crowded streets. Jakarta is hot, with a moist heat that tarnishes silver overnight, mildews your shoes and leaves a sinister white bloom on dark clothes. Foreigners often complain of the dirt, but this, I think, depends on whether you have got your eye into Asian cities. If your last town was Singapore, then, yes, Jakarta is dirty. If it was Bangkok, Rangoon or Calcutta, it is a miracle of cleanliness.

But the most persistent complaints are about Jakarta officialdom. To the complicated Dutch bureaucracy they inherited, the Indonesians have added an equally intricate one of their own, so that now they have more stringent immigration formalities, more insanely thorough customs examinations than any country I know; and worst of all, a persistent hangover of anti-foreign feeling. The only advice I can offer is keep your temper, understand the causes, and get out of Jakarta as quickly as possible, because in the rest of Indonesia you will find great courtesy and a genuinely gracious people.

When you travel in Java this courtesy may not be immediately apparent, for of all Indonesians the Javanese are the most reserved and complex. But their island is fascinating; it has produced Indonesia's highest culture, has been the scene of its great moments of history. Even before Hinduism reached Java in the fifteenth century, the Javanese had a civilization. In the museums you can see the ceramic and bronze relics from that period and the wonderful drums that were used for war and magic in the ancient animistic religion.

Hinduism filtered slowly into Java, but by the seventh century it flourished in an impressive empire. Around Jogjakarta, in Central Java, shadowed by the high, smoking volcano Merapi, are the extraordinary temples, stupas and tombs of that vast Hindu flowering.

Borobudur, a Buddhist stupa, carries in Asia the same artistic and religious authority as, say, Chartres does in Europe. It is a massive, circular monument, decorated with thousands of statues of Buddha and scenes from his life: dark, a little grim, extremely beautiful, set splendidly alone on a hilltop.

A more lively group are the temples called Prambanan, about ten miles out of Jogjakarta. The big central temple, dedicated to Lord Shiva and his consort Durga, reminds you of the great temples of Angkor. The towers rise with the same dizzying symmetry. Around the walls are the same friezes of wars and legends and gods, bas-reliefs with the same astonishing ease and vivid excitement. The sculptured decorations outside and the statues inside are of such consistent excellence that, again like Angkor, it is impossible to imagine so many skilled craftsmen at work in one place at the same time. Yet, scattered about the Jogjakarta plain are dozens of monuments—none the size of Prambanan or Borobudur, but of equal artistic merit—and even today the quietly elegant town of Jogjakarta is considered Indonesia's most important cultural center.

The last of the Hindu empires, whose capital was the fabulous lost city of Majapahit, rose in East Java, reached its height at the end of the fourteenth century and fell to the Islamic armies. The powerful Muslim sultanates brought their special refinements of manners and music to the palaces of Jogjakarta and Solo, but even they were conquered to a degree by a civilization already one of the highest in the world. And today, when you travel in Central Java and see the infinitely subtle and complex palace dancing, or hear the famous *gamelans* that provide the most impressive orchestral music in Asia, you will be witnessing arts that have flourished unbroken for more than a thousand years.

The Javanese are proudly conscious of their past. If you go shopping in Jakarta's huge cloth markets for batiks with an Indonesian friend, she may well point out one of the *kains*, stamped with big-headed, skinny-armed figures, and say, "That is a Majapahit design," or, "This one is copied from the old Solo palace *kains*."

Often I have asked Indonesians if they are Javanese, and they have replied, "No, I am Sundanese" (though Sunda is only the western province of Java), because a distant time ago Sunda was a separate kingdom, with its own rulers, conquests and culture. The stories that the Indonesians know best are ancient, mythological legends of a religion that most of them no longer practice, and the most popular and universal entertainment—the shadow play—concerns itself chiefly with Javanese epics which are more than two thousand years old.

It is easy to understand how this deep pride of civilization, of ancient origins, was profoundly offended by three centuries of Dutch colonial rule. The nationalist revolution that followed World War II was most bitterly fought, and is still very much in Javanese minds. The first thing that they will tell you about the island of Bangka, for instance, is not that it is extremely rich in tin, but that it was the place where the revolutionary leaders were imprisoned; before they describe the beauties of the famous resort of Lake Toba, they will tell you that President Sukarno was once kept under house arrest there.

All of Indonesia's names have been changed back to the old forms, and even though people comment that the "Wild Man of Kalimantan" doesn't really sound right to people who have grown up hearing Borneo, or that Maluku lacks the romantic associations of the old Spice Islands, still, to the Indonesians these names are signs of their new independence.

Foreigners who visit Java are often puzzled and irritated by the nationalistic clamor in Indonesian politics and by the antiforeign feeling in daily life. Still, these can be sympathetically explained: economically, Indonesia is not yet free of the Dutch; also, its leaders have not completed the immense task of creating a genuinely representative government, one that will bring a sense of national identity to all of the country's scattered islands. At the same time the government must somehow manage to run the country with a minimum of trained men and little money.

Indonesia's prime minister, Ali Sastromidjojo, once gave an illustration of his country's problem. If you write a letter to someone in Indonesia, he said, it will probably get there, though the service won't be as fast or as certain as in some other countries; but then, he asked, have you ever thought of the problems of running a postal system in which most of your mail carriers, sorters and postmen can't read or write? Perhaps the fairest way to judge Indonesia is to realize that conditions are infinitely better than they were six years ago, much better than two years ago, and will continue to improve with luck, help and a measure of peace. Meanwhile, once you leave Jakarta, you will find all the pleasures of Javanese life untouched by political bitterness.

Java is an incredibly beautiful island—green, rich, with a manicured landscape reaching from the coastal plains up to the central spine of mountains. I remember, on my first drive into the Sunda hills, being astonished by rice fields at different stages of growth—some just planted, some ready to be harvested, some half grown. With Java's climate and soil, farmers can be casual in their farming methods. An American agricultural expert told me he had tried to show Javanese farmers how to spray their rice crops, to save twenty-five per cent from insect damage. One of the farmers remarked, most politely, "We need not trouble, seventy-five per cent of the crop is enough."

In the pleasant hill towns of Bogor or Bandung you can sample many of the activities of Javanese life, with a degree of Western comfort. Often as you walk down the road of an evening you hear music or drumming from a private house or a compound. It is perfectly all right to stand behind the invited guests and watch the show. Usually the show's an all-night shadow play, the most popular Javanese entertainment for family occasions such as birth or a circumcision ceremony. A big, white sheet forms a screen; behind it a huge fire is kept burning, or, in more modern compounds, oil lamps or electric bulbs. A number of men operate the puppets (characters from old legends), cut from stiff, translucent leather with movable arms and legs. An old man sits at the side chanting the story, and with a wonderful range of voice delivers the brave speeches of the heroes, intones the sinister plottings of the demons, and occasionally recapitulates for late-comers.

The audience crouches on the ground or sits on steps, walls, or even in the branches of trees nearby. Children listen for a while, fall asleep, suddenly wake to the drumming and shouts of a battle scene and run out to the street stalls for peanuts, or a favorite pink sirupy drink, or to smoke a cigarette that smells like carnations. All through the night the big, dreamlike shadows move across the screen; enemies are vanquished with jerky movements of puppet arms, kings and queens move stiffly in procession with flickering retinues of horses, soldiers, palanquins.

Or perhaps you will happen on the doll plays, a more sophisticated form of puppet drama in which the puppeteer, a skilled artist, sits in full view with his dolls beside him. The green trunk of a banana tree before him acts as a stage upon which the grotesque little figures dance—so flexible, so full of emotion, so graceful, that you must look around the audience at the end of an act to readjust your sense of reality.

If the puppeteer sees foreigners in the crowd he usually introduces an extra flourish into one of the comedy scenes.

"Do you speak English?" one clown asks another.

"I speak English very good."

"Speak then."

The second clown counts to four in Dutch.

The first then gabbles in Javanese, "That isn't English, that's the language of the demons!" The crowd screams with delighted laughter.

In small towns and villages, you may see plays performed by traveling companies or hear shrill, sweet-voiced Javanese singers accompanied by an instrument like a zither. Or you can shop in the bazaars for the beautiful, dark Jogjakarta silver, the old and new batiks, or simply enjoy the pleasures of what the Indonesians call "walking-walking," a kind of aimless wandering about to see what people are doing, view the country, admire the sunset behind a volcano, stop at a tiny wayside restaurant for a couple of sticks of saté (small, spiced bits of meat grilled on a bamboo skewer) and, finally, just talk and talk and talk.

In many ways Sumatra is the most exciting of all the Indonesian islands. Large parts of Sumatra have never been explored, even by Indonesians, and the island has a special invigorating temper, an atmosphere at once bustling and assured.

This one island, about the size of California and with a population of twelve million, accounts for over half the wealth of Indonesia. From the central swamps and jungles huge American refineries extract oil; in the northern coastal plains enormous plantations produce tobacco, rubber, palm oil and tea. But vast areas of the mountainous east coast are virtually unexploited; few people live there and fewer travel through. The heavy jungles are ruled by elephants and rhinoceroses, while tigers and jaguars wander in the grasslands and orangutans swing ominously overhead.

South Sumatra produced one of the earliest grandeurs of Indonesian history, the great eighth-century empire of Sri Vijaya which was centered around the famous city of Palembang. Virtually nothing remains of the ancient capital—an occasional bronze figure of a Hindu god, relics of a demolished tomb, a fragment of ancient script in a palmyra-leaf book—that is all; but Palembang itself is still an important center commercially, booming with the money and increased employment that the oil refineries bring. American hotels, Dutch hotels, Chinese hotels, Arab and Chinese shops and businesses. Theaters showing Indian movies, Chinese, American or Indonesian movies. A busy river port (the wide Musi cuts the city in half) with steamers fussing their way up the seven-hour trip from the sea, and an active river life of smaller boats, thousands of families living in houseboats, and an occasional, brightly painted wooden barge decorated with colored lights and lanterns—pleasure boats from which you hear singing and bursts of laughter as you pass in your launch, and, of course, many floating Chinese restaurants. Close beyond it all, not yet conquered, are the wild marshes and the jungle.

It is all undeniably lively, but a long way from the ancient center of Buddhism that boasted the biggest university in Asia and drew scholars from China, Ceylon and India. About the only memories of the great lost empire remain in the place names, in the armbands of the local soldiers (the Sri Vijayan battalion) and in a particularly pleasing dance that is considered necessary to any delicately brought-up lady's education—the Gending Sri Vijaya.

A group of four or six girls performs this for you as a welcoming gesture to a Sumatran house. With flowers in their hair and long curling strips of gold attached to each fingernail, with the smooth grace that Indonesians seem to possess as a birthright, the girls dance out the meaning of the song. "We have heard for a month of your coming, O Prince of Sri Vijaya. . . ." With a strange subdued longing the girls move their hands, clasping and spreading them in impatience. "We have watched for your coming from every direction. . . ." The hands with their curving gold tips flick first one way then the other, the little gold hearts hanging like charms from the fingernails flash and tremble with the movement. "We have made many preparations. . . ." The lightest, most economical of gestures indicate the flowers in the hair, the dusting of powder on the face, the eyes elongated with kohl, the jewels, the dress. "We await your order . . . we will prepare anything you want, the highest or the lowest. . . ." Fluttering hands, controlled swaying body, gently rhythmic bare feet—all create the pattern of gracious humility. At last the honored guest has come. The lead dancer fetches a silver tray holding the beautifully carved bowls and pots of betel ingredients. Her eyes are almost closed, looking at the ground (it would, of course, be too bold for a young girl to look an exalted guest full in the face), and she places the tray before you. Two of the others glide up with spittoons. They all dance modestly back to the group, and with that your proper and formal welcome is complete.

The most vigorously modern city in Sumatra is Medan in the north, the island's leading town. The streets are wide and clean, the houses look new and have pleasantly disregarded the old, solid, four-square colonial architecture. Even the names of the bus companies—the Atom and Arrow buses, the King Kong Express, and my favorite, the *Beta Hamu*, or Let's Go Bus Company—contribute to a feeling of push and vitality entirely uncharacteristic of equatorial lands.

Because Medan is so close to Malaya, the city has taken on some of what a Medanese acquaintance described to me as "the knowledge of jazz and night living" of Singapore. The most popular dance, for instance, is the *serampang duabelas* (twelve step) which is particularly daring because a man invites a girl to dance alone with him. Another favorite is considered pretty fast because in it a girl hopes her young man will come back to her village even though "he is leaving for further studies at the university" and while there may get trapped by city pleasures.

Only the big Medan mosque, with its walls of cream-colored wash and pale-blue tiles, and the yellow gingerbread fantasy of the Sultan of Deli's palace give the city a touch of old-fashioned Oriental exoticism. Foreigners insist that Medan is the best place in Indonesia to live. You can get things *done*, they tell you. The people are open and expressive—very different from the reserved Javanese. They are experimental, willing to try out new ideas, anxious to travel. Once when I mentioned this to a Javanese friend, she nodded distantly, and said, with a slight touch of disdain, "Yes, the Bataks are known to be very wandering and talking types."

Only a couple of hours away from Medan is one of Indonesia's most famous beauty spots—cold green Lake Toba, set in high austere country like a lunar landscape, a harsh northern beauty

150

of sharp volcanic hills, sheer cliffs and the crystal air of the high country. Far to the north live the fierce Aché warriors, who claimed to have enlisted the aid of whole graveyards of ghosts in their battles against the Dutch and insisted that the corpses of the people killed in those battles never decayed but gave off the aroma of flowers.

Beyond Toba, to the south, are the Batak villages with their extraordinary houses with wildly soaring roofs, and beyond them the tangled mountain country, massive, cut by high rift valleys and complicated with virtually uncharted jungles, magnificent to look at and frightening to get a flat tire in.

Relatively few people visit this part of the country, but anywhere in Indonesia you will hear stories of Menangkabau. The people are so clever, you are told, that Bukittinggi, the Menangkabau capital, is the only place in the islands where a Chinese merchant is not assured of success—the local Sumatrans are too sharp. The government and politics of Indonesia, even though Jakarta is their center, are studded with people from Menangkabau. Almost every significant leader, except President Sukarno, comes from Bukittinggi or one of the neighboring villages.

The most popular explanation for this amazing output of talent and brains is that Menangkabau is one of the few genuine matriarchies in the world. Women own and administer the property. When a woman marries, her bridegroom comes to live in her house. Her children take their maternal name, and most significant of all—when a boy is between fifteen and seventeen he is expected to leave home and family and set out to seek his fortune. This custom, they say, accounts for the drive, resourcefulness and eminence of Menangkabau men.

Bukittinggi itself, a mountain town of singularly insouciant charm, is dramatically set between two volcanoes, one extinct,

151

the other active. The Menangkabau description is, "Merapi is sleeping, but its dreams of the active one are bad"—it puffs and fumes from time to time. The people of Bukittinggi prosaically call it Buffalo Gully because its deep pastures make such rich grazing, and because this is supposed to be the site of a legendary Bukittinggi battle. In the days of the Sri Vijayan empire, the fighters of south Sumatra challenged the mountain people to battle. But instead the mountain people persuaded them to decide the issue by a fight between two buffaloes.

The rich southerners chose an enormous animal, a mother who would be particularly fierce because she was separated from her young; the mountain people chose a small calf to whose budding horns they attached a sharp dagger. In the battle the southerners' cow, seeing no danger from the mountain calf, stood still and allowed the calf to gambol to her side and attempt to suckle. Immediately, of course, the dagger pushed deep into the cow's belly and killed her. The victory went to the mountain people and ever since they have been called Menangkabau—a slight corruption of Winning Water Buffalo—and their ingenuity and independence have been established.

In Bukittinggi one has the sensation of living in a light of peculiar clarity, very dry, very uncompromising. Each morning and evening one of the volcanoes turns slowly purple with shadow. The odd acoustics of Buffalo Gully bring isolated sounds from the villages far down at the foot of the cliff, or the rustle of monkeys swinging fussily through the trees, and usually there is a distant drumming from one of the mosques or from the market because the Menangkabau people have a special fondness for drums and use them to announce everything from Islam's five daily calls to prayer to a demonstration of a hair oil by a traveling medicine man.

During the day the market place acquires a pleasant frivolity from the huge colored umbrellas over the stalls. There you can buy silk and gold or silver formal sarongs or the agonizingly intricate filigree ornaments made by local silversmiths. From the painted houses with their double and treble roofs curving up in spires like a buffalo's horns, whole families walk to the Bukittinggi market with their fruit and vegetables. The women wear the long Sumatran tunic over their sarongs, and the men are dressed in chic ankle-length trousers made in batiks of bold brown, blue and white designs.

An entertaining way to spend an idle evening anywhere in Indonesia, but particularly in Bukittinggi, is to find the local group of *penchak* dancers and ask them to put on a show. *Penchak*, a tense, rapid, stylized performance somewhere between a fight and a dance, is one of Indonesia's best diversions. This, combined with the Indonesian passion for clubs (there are music, dance, football, religious clubs, and more mysterious ones with names like The Revolutionary Young Men's Art and Charity Society, and the Victorious Religion and Rhythm Club), means that virtually every village in Indonesia has its *penchak* group. It combines the excitement of a prize fight (without its cruelty) with the aesthetic satisfactions of the dance (without its abstractions).

Before I went to Sumatra I had seen *penchak* only in Bali, where it is so much more dance than fight that often an expert will perform a solo, eliminating the idea of conflict entirely, to an accompaniment of drums and cymbals. In Bukittinggi it is deadly serious, performed in a silence broken only by the claps, shouts and whispering feet of the dancers. Wearing loose black trousers and tunics, they make a deep obeisance before their

153

teacher, sink to their knees and touch his hand and then their own heart and head. They circle the dance area with a kind of excited caution. They attack with a lightning kick, the blurred arc of an arm. Still perfectly in control they wrestle with a subtle and wicked skill on the ground. They make fantastic leaps. A brief unexpected thrust will bring a dagger rattling to the ground. A headdress will fly off, a tunic be covered with dust. Yet it never loses the quality of a dance. The teacher sits rigidly watching every move, ready to stop the fight the second he feels that the hearts of the dancers have become "blinded by the heat of the dance" and that they might overdo it and injure each other.

After such a performance we asked the chief *penchak* dancer to show us the most difficult movements and hand gestures so that we could watch with more intelligence.

"I can't do that," he replied, embarrassed.

"Why not?"—Indonesians are usually most accommodating about explaining their arts.

"Well," he said seriously, "to show you the hardest gestures of *penchak* would involve killing a man."

We explained that we wanted only to understand what the movements were, and when with a rather nervous partner he slowly demonstrated, we realized that with Bukittinggi *penchak* you could indeed kill a man. It needs two almost invisible hand gestures and one accurate and vicious kick. The whole thing takes only three seconds.

I suppose everyone has a dream trip he plans to take when he has money enough and time. Mine is a very unhurried wandering in a large sailboat through the islands of Indonesia, returning to places I have particularly liked, exploring islands that sound interesting, or which have good beaches, or pleasing legends, or simply attractive names. I would certainly spend some time, for instance, on an island off the west coast of Sumatra called Nias, a weird, forbidding island that maintains, almost unchanged, its New Stone Age culture. From the ocean you can see fortress villages built on hills and roads of great stone steps leading up to them. The island is studded with mysterious stone monuments, enormous slabs six feet high—altars perhaps from some ancient sacrificial rite?—and used by the islanders as measures for high-jumping contests that are part of their religious ceremonies. If you ask the meaning of the high-jump competitions, they tell you only, "Power belongs to the man who can jump high."

If you press the point you are told a legend of the days when Sumatra was a patchwork of warring kingdoms and Nias was frequently raided for slaves. "To jump high brought a man safety. When an enemy approached there was no time for anyone to put down a ladder from the houses" (which were, and still are, built on stilts), "he had only time enough to leap directly into a house and save his life."

I would try to get to Nias for one of their feast days, to see the shuffling, leaping dances performed in a most extraordinary costume—a flared, seventeenth-century Portuguese jacket worn over a G-string fastened with a colossal button which is covered with the teeth of wild animals. The dancer's props are a long spear and a wooden shield carved to look like an alligator.

My island hopping would, of course, take me to Kalimantan (Borneo) and the little kingdom of Pontianak. From there a wide river leads up to the Dyak country with its special tribal civilization and its inquisitive, friendly people. On the trip inland you see villages of river houses backed by the jungle; acres of blue water hyacinths drifting down to the sea and the long river canoes speeding between villages. In the Dyak country the

155

people wear short tight sarongs fastened with belts of silver coins; they don't trust paper money and on the few occasions they cannot barter for their needs they use Mexican or U.S. silver dollars. The men of the village greet you and with correct Dyak formality offer you *air minum* or *susu*—literally, "water" or "milk"—but whichever you choose, you will still be served wine. Before you drink, you will be invited to walk up a tilted tree trunk, into the house of the chief of the Dyak village, properly seated on the floor; then with etiquette satisfied, conversation and questions begin. All this, of course, is on the southeast coast of Kalimantan —a place that is relatively simple to reach.

For more rugged adventuring, you can take the long journey north to the wild and unexplored mountains of central Kalimantan, to the unpredictable country of the hill tribes.

Eastward the island of Sulawesi (Celebes) lies like an eccentric orchid between Kalimantan and Malaku. Makassar, the capital, sounds wonderfully exotic, but turns out to be rather dowdy. It has, however, one moment of the day when it is romantically beautiful: immediately after sunset the fleets of square-sailed fishing boats come in between the islands of Makassar Bay; the beaches turn gold and the lichened walls of eighteenth-century Fort Rotterdam become an odd purplish velvet; the women along the sea wall, their heads covered with lace and muslin shawls, their faces powdered dead white for beauty, stand in that moment of early evening to watch the boats come in.

Makassar's markets and docks have particular exuberance because the people of Sulawesi have the most uninhibited sense of color of any Indonesians. In most of the country the subdued batiks of Java make up the smart dress, but in Makassar the men lounge around the quays in fabulous sarongs of fuchsia and turquoise. They pedal briskly down the streets on bicycles or pedicabs in heavy, luminous silks checked with yellow and pink, striped with purple and orange. They pay up to forty dollars for a three-yard length of their own brilliant materials—even the poorest coolie seems to own at least one such sarong—and even the chic Jogjakarta styles are too tame for the gaudy Sulawesi taste. Up country, the Toraja tribes express their intoxication with color in their short bright cotton loincloths and the wooden walls of their fantastic horned houses which they paint red and white and green and decorate with buffalo heads.

One of the most attractive island journeys is also one of the most accessible: a few days on a coastal freighter takes you along the north shore of Java, calling at the charming port towns with the magical names—Cheribon, Semarang, Surabaya. After Surabaya comes the special and enchanted island of Bali.

Indonesians are apt to be both puzzled and irritated by the foreigner's enthusiasm for Bali. Often when I have talked about that incredible island with Indonesians (admittedly, with a rather uncritical excitement) I have noticed that they get the same look of exasperated boredom that Indians get if you rave about the Taj Mahal. They point out that other parts of Indonesia are more beautiful (which is true), that Sundanese music is more highly developed, that the palace dancing of Solo and Jogjakarta is more exquisite, that Bali has no literature, has produced virtually no intellectuals (all equally true). But the Balinese have a charm so overwhelming that if I had to suggest only one place in Asia to visit, it would certainly be Bali.

By now Balinese music and dancing are both famous, and to a smaller extent so is Balinese sculpture; but what makes Bali so much more than simply a living museum of impressive artistic achievement is the accessible and relaxed appeal of the people—impossible to describe if you haven't been there, impossible to forget if you have.

Once I asked a Balinese friend why visitors were so impressed with his island.

He said, "How can I answer? That is a foreigner's question."

"But you must have wondered," I insisted, "especially since so many tourists come here?"

"Perhaps," he suggested doubtfully, "they are unhappy in their own country? Perhaps that is why they travel? Balinese are more calm in their minds."

And, certainly, it is an extraordinary experience to live in a place where you are surrounded entirely by happy people.

Beyond Bali the long broken arc of islands continues all the way to Irian (New Guinea) and eventually to Australia. Each island has its special distinction and its special attraction. Even anthropologists and archaeologists have scarcely begun the enthralling business of exploring those islands, and for the traveler there are virtually no guides except their own sense of adventure. For instance, Lombok, next to Bali, is odd because it marks the line where Asia stops and Australia begins, in flora and fauna at least, where tigers and man apes vanish, and Australia's cockatoos and marsupials begin.

Komodo, further to the east, is perhaps best known as the only place in the world where "dragons" still exist—actually they are enormous, prehistoric-looking lizards. Sumba is famous for the great herds of horses that roam the island and which have so affected the local culture that for ceremonial occasions and dances the people decorate themselves with horsetails and perform strange stamping movements punctuated with a sort of whinnying shout. Flores is known for its many-colored lakes and the mysterious ceremonies of magic that are connected with them.

I suppose one could continue to sail among the islands of Indonesia for years, always discovering new places and customs, never exhausting the possibilities and the interest of the country. An American friend of mine who was soon to leave Indonesia once listed for me the things she would miss most: the sight of schoolchildren walking down the road in the rain, each solemnly carrying a large banana leaf as an umbrella; the people bathing in the rivers—the Indonesian skin, extraordinarily lovely at any time, acquires a startling glow with the water and the evening light; the offhand grace of a Balinese woman tying up her hair in a faded towel; the Sundanese hillsides sculptured with huge green rice terraces; the young men of a village tensely crouching around a cockfight; a farmer in a wide palm hat with two sheaves of rice slung from a pole across his shoulder, trotting with that special bouncing gait that makes the rice shiver golden in the sun; the supreme elegance of an old Jogjakarta lady, gray hair knotted high, shoulders a little stooped, the knife-edged pleats of her *kain* fanning out, as she walks very slowly down the road.

After you have traveled in Indonesia there will always be moments and memories and pictures in your mind that capture the special quality of the country—a mixture of simplicity and charm, cultivation and a quite unconscious beauty.

BALI
the happy land

Ever SINCE I FIRST WENT TO THE ISLAND OF
Bali, like almost everyone else that has ever visited it, I have remained enchanted by the place, the people and their life. Of
course, Bali is only one tiny island in the archipelago of Indonesia, part of the nation, but so different in mood, in history, religion and way of living, that I think it deserves a separate
chapter.

People who knew Bali "in the old days" (with Bali, "the old
days" mean anything from the prewar years to a few months
ago) and who have revisited the island will often tell you that
Bali has changed. They always say it with some element of distress, with a sense of something precious and romantic lost. Well,
Bali *has* changed—and will, I hope—continue to change. It
would be a dead and boring civilization if it didn't. But Bali
always seems to change within its own rules, within its own particular view of the world and how to live in it. The thing that
is lost is not some virtue of Balinese life, but the foreigner's private
dream of how Bali *should* act and live, some conventionally storybook version of that celebrated island. Personally, Bali's changes
over the years nearly always delight me; they give an added
variety to an already wonderfully various place. And then, I
have so strong a faith in the vitality and integrity of Bali's
special civilization that I feel they will always be able to transform
any influences from the outside world that they may adopt or

be forced to accept into something intimately their own. When, for instance, the Communist party wanted to establish a branch office in Bali, the people of Den Pasar, the capital, welcomed them most politely. But after several months of propaganda and vigorous campaigning, they found that they had enlisted only two Balinese to their cause—both of them known to be chronic malcontents. The Communists decided to postpone their work in Bali until the people were "better prepared" to understand the new doctrine.

Actually, Bali has a well-functioning social system of its own —again, uniquely Balinese, full of contradictions and odd local arrangements, but apparently nicely adapted to their temperament. Although they maintain an elaborate hierarchy of rajas, princes and lesser aristocracy, many of them rich (by Balinese standards) and powerful, the structure of their society is really closer to a socialistic welfare state. The Council of Rajas in consultation, sometimes, with elected representatives of local governments, make most of the decisions that concern the whole island. Village administration is handled by a series of "clubs" that function something like co-operatives. There will always be, for example, a "club" to harvest the crops of any village area because that is considered a communal affair and everyone must pitch in and help everyone else to be sure that no individual crop is ruined by unexpected storms or rain. There are "clubs" to arrange a village festival, to organize the markets, as well as the more familiar music and dance and athletic clubs that provide much of village entertainment.

Any of these clubs is usually advised by one or a group of "elders," people of the village who have in some informal but accepted way acquired the reputation for wisdom in this or that matter. The Balinese perfectly understand the principles of democratic election, but seldom bother with its forms. I never saw anything but the vaguest gesture toward electioneering in Bali. It is simply "known" which man would be best for which job in local governments, and if he can be persuaded to take office (something that the Balinese don't much like), everyone is happy and there seems to be virtually no disagreement. Of course this sort of arrangement is both possible and sensible in Bali's conglomeration of small agricultural communities where there is little mobility and where, consequently, people know their fellow villagers all their life and can make a reasonable judgment of character.

On national issues and in general elections any Balinese who "feels" twenty-one years old votes. The Balinese are wonderfully careless about age. If you ask a Balinese child his age, he may reply in a speculative voice, "About fifteen?" If you suggest that he couldn't possibly be fifteen, he looks much younger, he will not be disconcerted, will probably not even be much interested, but is apt to answer politely, "Do you think so? Well, perhaps I am ten or twelve?"

Bali, like India, has its distinctions of caste in the conventional Hindu pattern; however, here too the Balinese have their own peculiarly flexible arrangement. Unlike India, there are no Untouchables or Harijans. A woman takes on the caste of her husband whether she marries above or below her station. Except for the priests, who must be Brahmins, caste does not determine professions or occupations. Few of the rarefied tabus of caste and religion remain in Bali—a Balinese, for instance, is not a vegetarian; he eats all kinds of meat including pork and often beef as well. Cows are not sacred, and if they are protected it is only because they are useful draft animals. Altogether it is a most relaxed form of Hinduism and seems to work very pleasantly to the satisfaction of everybody.

One drawback to Bali, and one factor that may be responsible for the disappointment that some travelers revisiting Bali feel, is the look and the life of the towns. When you leave Bali you have in your mind the infinite appeal of the villages and countryside of the island. It then comes as something of a shock to find that your first view of Bali when you return is either Den Pasar, if you come by air, or Singharaja if you arrive by ship. Both are messy, sprawling little towns with a few crowded bazaars where the Chinese and Indians have shops, an indifferent hotel, some government administration buildings and entirely undistinguished architecture. Singharaja is the port town on the north coast of Bali. In contrast with the rest of the island it is a bustling metropolis with most of its activity centered on the shipping and the docks. It has a certain excitement in the sight of the many types of craft, in the evocative names of their destinations—Celebes, New Guinea, Borneo—and in its *pasar malam* or "evening bazaar." This turns out to be more of a fiesta than a bazaar, a place for singing and dancing and puppet shows as well as an occasion to wander among the stalls of batiks and silver from Java, or bright silks from Makassar, or Chinese porcelain or ivory from Burma. Here many dashing new styles originate. It was in Singharaja's *pasar malam* that the popular *kebyar* dance, formerly reserved for men, was first performed by a duet of girls. Here, too, the latest Balinese craze for the *joget bum-bum* originated. The *joget* is, in any case, a flirt dance in which the girl dancer chooses from the audience men to partner her in the increasingly swift and intricate steps. She invites them with amazingly suggestive tremblings of an eyebrow, and then proceeds to outdance each one and send him back defeated. In the racy style of Singharaja, however, the *jogets* changed the traditional music of the bamboo orchestra (xylophones made of graded, hollow bamboo stems, and bamboo flutes) to a faster and more obviously rhythmic cadence, and intensified the amorousness of the dance to such an extent that fights would break out among the men in the audience out of jealousy for the girl dancers.

Den Pasar, at the southern end of the island, is quieter even though it has Bali's only industry (a canning factory owned by a Chinese). It has, besides, a museum (built by the Dutch) which is sometimes open, and easy access to Bali's best beaches. However, my advice about both these towns, as with Jakarta, is to get out of them as soon as possible. The dubious advantages of second-rate hotels are a small thing to give up in exchange for the exhilarating charm of Balinese living, and the dependable beauty of Bali's countryside.

When first I was in Bali, six years ago, I remarked to a Balinese friend—an old and distinguished man in the village where I stayed—that he should travel and see the world beyond his island. With surprise he replied, "I have already traveled. I went to Java when I was young."

"But that's not very far," I insisted. "Java is your closest neighbor."

"It is far enough," he said with finality. "I could see from the faces of the people that they had unhappy hearts. Their rice fields were not as beautiful as ours, and their dancing did not belong to everybody. When I came home I knew that Bali was the best place in the world."

After a good deal of traveling on several continents, I find that I agree with him.

The tiny island, among the smallest in the Indonesian archipelago, has been admired for the beauty of its people and its countryside, for the vitality of its arts, for the gentleness and charm of the Balinese nature, even for its religious exuberance. Even the most casual tourist can hardly fail to be pleased by the Balinese countryside. From the wonderful sandy beaches of Kuta, and the strange, stark tableland of Bali's southern promontory, the island extends northward in graded planes of rice fields and coconut groves—the typical tropical landscape—to the windy mountains of central Bali and the sharp cliffs jutting along the north shore.

They tell you in Bali that the island has just enough of everything—enough jungles in the west for tiger-shooting; one live volcano and the high improbable perfection of the extinct Gunung Agung; a couple of lakes between the volcanoes; pine forests on the slopes of the hills; and then, with a pleasing inevitability, the rice fields and the coconut groves again.

But the thing I came to like best of all when I lived in Bali was the extraordinary pleasure, diversity and excitement of Balinese village life. In the years since I have often tried to analyze just what is so appealing about day-to-day living in Bali. The people are friendly and have a sense of humor combined with a kind of tough realism that I like. The pleasures of dancing, music, gambling and cockfighting can be endlessly absorbing. Life, even without electricity, radios, newspapers, running water and other trappings of civilization, can be extremely comfortable. In a Balinese village one seems to be busy all day without time or inclination even to read. I gossiped with friends, went for long walks with the village children through Bali's incredibly beautiful rice fields, and in the evenings there was nearly always a dance, a play or puppet show within walking distance of the village. And somehow all of this seemed to give Bali the most attractive life in the world.

Of course I went back to Ubud, the village where I had lived before, to spend a few days with my best friends there—Chokorda Agung and his two wives. (Chokorda is a Balinese title meaning, roughly, "prince," and second only to raja.) I had sent no warning message, not even a letter, but simply arrived one afternoon.

Chokorda Agung was sitting in a small pavilion atop the wall of his outer courtyard, watching the village world go by and chatting with his cousin and a couple of friends who were on their way to Den Pasar. In the usual Balinese way, they had stopped by for a visit and an exchange of local news.

A stocky, jolly man, Chokorda Agung scrambled down from the wall, laughing and calling out explanations to his friends. "I was wondering when you would return to Ubud," he said to me. "You are married, I hear, and you have a child. A son? Very good. Your old house has others living in it, but you will stay with us until we can find you another."

"This is only for a few days," I protested.

"That is what you said the last time. Come and see the wives."

We walked through the courtyards of his *puri*—palace, the literal translation, makes it sound pretentious. Still, it is a big compound in accordance with his rank, and represents the wealth of many rice fields. I remembered the time many years ago, when we sat in his wall pavilion looking out over the *puri*, which was extraordinarily lovely in the dark blue twilight of late evening, and he asked me casually, "Do your Indian princes have such palaces?"

I had been at a loss to describe the obviously unimagined richness, size and grandeur of Indian palaces, and had answered at last, "Not so beautiful as this."

In each courtyard of the *puri* there are two or three pavilions, all set on platforms a couple of feet high, all with thatched roofs. Some are open on all sides with carved and gilded pillars at each corner to support the roof; others have varying numbers of walls, sometimes only one, with palm-leaf screens for the other sides that can be put up against the rain. We walked through the big bare courtyard of stamped earth where they hold dances, using the tall red-and-white gate covered with carvings of Hindu gods and heroes. We turned through the cannas and jasmine bushes of the inner courtyards, between the frangipani trees from which the *puri* boys pick flowers to tuck behind an ear, past the music pavilion and the tooth-filing pavilion, where, with proper ceremonies in the correct Balinese way, a man must have his teeth filed—it is a dreaded misfortune to die before your teeth are filed and thus lose your chance of peace in after-death. We came at last to the innermost courtyard. There one of the wives sat on the floor at a hand loom, weaving dark red cloth with the Balinese designs of stylized flowers and stripes. The younger wife came running out from behind the house, winding her hair into the loose, haphazard loop that married women wear. It was an ordinary enough Balinese scene, but once again I was caught in the special Balinese magic, the particular grace of even the most uncalculated movement, a quality of easy acceptance of their surroundings, a contentment with life.

We sat in the wives' pavilion facing the garden, which was framed between the gold rosettes of the pillars. I told the wives politely that they hadn't changed at all, were still as beautiful as ever. One of them stared at me thoughtfully. "Well," she said, "*you* look older. Your hair is turning white." I remembered, then, that no conventional foreign manners will ever force a compliment from a Balinese, a very relaxing idea once you get used to it.

We went on to catch up on six years of Ubud activities, of births and marriages and deaths, of who had built new houses, written compositions for the music society, bought or sold rice fields, painted attractive pictures. We drank palm beer and the sweet black Balinese coffee. We talked about Hinduism, the new temple in the village, the coming festivals and cockfights.

As usual an intermittent stream of people ambled through the *puri*. The Balinese have no particular sense of privacy, and anyone going to a neighboring house is likely to use the *puri* as a short cut. If they have time to spare they will perch on the steps and listen to the conversation. They will sit at a lower level as a mark of deference to the Chokorda, but think nothing of joining the talk. Once, long ago, I tried to persuade my houseboys, when they were serving meals, not to join in the dinner-table conversation, especially if guests were present. This was met with a puzzled interest. Before becoming entangled in what I knew would be senseless explanations, I added a phrase that I found very useful in Bali; "In my country, this is *adat*." *Adat* means, vaguely, traditional custom, and the Balinese have a respect even for foreign *adat*, however unnatural it may seem. "All right," one of them agreed seriously, "if that is what you wish. We will correct them only if they are wrong."

"No, no," I said, "not even then. Especially not then."

"But if they make a mistake they will *want* to be told. It will make them happy."

"It will make them angry," I said.

"If you get angry," one of the boys remarked with a sort of complacent instructiveness, "you quickly get old. That is a Balinese proverb."

I abandoned my effort, and mealtime conversations were far more entertaining as a result.

Often, as people went through the *puri*, Chokorda Agung would call out the perennial Balinese inquiries, "Whence are you coming?" and "Where are you going?"—and the answers would be, "I am coming from the fields and go now to the river to bathe," or "from Pliatan where my sister is sick and I'm going home now." Very soon I reacquired the comforting feeling of knowing what was going on in Ubud. I found myself interested again in who had lost money at the trained-cricket fights, in somebody's flooded irrigation ditch (a serious matter because the irrigation of the rice fields as well as the harvesting of the grain is a community affair), in a new litter of pigs, in the fact that a young man had been seen to take a long detour to pass the house of a pretty girl.

Soon the *puri* children came chattering home from school, running barefoot through the courtyards, swinging their copybooks in bamboo straps. Later, women wandered through on their way to visit friends. A cowherd came past with two of the caramel-colored, fairy-story cows of Bali that look almost like deer; he was taking them to graze on a strip of good grass along the outer wall of the *puri*. In the early evening a small boy carrying a long stick with a white flag at the end guided his ducks back to their shed; every morning, like all Balinese duck owners, he led them out, as if they were sheep, to the flooded rice fields where they swam about and fed. A foreigner once told me that he had hired a car to take him to Den Pasar for an appointment. He was in a hurry and became annoyed when the car had to crawl behind a flock of ducks waddling across a narrow bridge. "Sound the horn," the foreigner ordered the Balinese driver.

"That will distress the boy for no reason," the Balinese replied. "The ducks are walking as fast as they can."

After we had talked for some time one of the wives excused

herself to supervise the cooking of the evening meal. Later a little
girl came by with a shallow basket balanced on her head. She
placed tiny palm-leaf trays of rice and flowers here and there in
the *puri,* some on the ground to pacify the spirits of the earth,
some in tall stone shrines for the spirits of the air, some in the
notches of trees for the spirits of growing things. The Balinese
are Hindus, but cautiously keep in the good graces of their
original animistic deities as well.

Eventually Chokorda Agung jumped up and announced that
we should pay our respects to the other Chokordas. Agung's old
uncle who lived in the adjoining *puri* was sitting in his living
pavilion, listening to the story of someone's troubles. Most likely
the man would come to live in the *puri* and be supported by the
old Chokorda until he got back on his feet. In Bali, if you have
money you expect to support a number of people—relatives and
friends—who are in difficulties. One of the aspects of Western
life that most upsets the Balinese is what they describe as the
"loneliness of misfortune"—the unwillingness to receive or give
help casually. I asked a Balinese friend what would happen if a
man got into trouble through his own foolishness; if, for instance, he sold his fields and went off to Den Pasar and lost all
his money gambling.

"He would walk back to his village. Nowhere in Bali is too far
to walk within a few days."

"But when he reached his own village—suppose he was a bad
man and had no friends?"

"Nobody in Bali is without friends," was the astonished
answer. "They would help him."

Chokorda Agung's old uncle politely greeted us and almost at
once announced his chief news to me. He was eighty years old,
but last year he had married again and now he had a three-month-

old baby. "It is a good sign that an old man should have a baby. It means that the era of Kali in which we have been living is near its end. Wars and fighting will diminish and a new period of peace and fresh life will begin."

We next called on Chokorda Rahi, who is about sixty and one of the handsomest men I ever saw. He was performing his daily devotions before a small shrine at the back of the courtyard. After a few minutes he came out formally dressed in an elegant *kain* —the straight, three-yard length of batik tightly tied at the waist; he was bare-chested and wore a smartly folded headcloth embellished with hibiscus.

He called to his wife to bring out the sweet, bland rice wine that she makes herself, and while we sipped it slowly Chokorda Rahi, who forty years ago had been one of Bali's best dancers, brought me up on the local dance news. I told him that what I most wanted to see in Ubud was the *gabor,* which I remembered as the most beautiful dance I had ever seen.

"But we no longer have a *gabor.* It finished three years ago."

"Oh, what a pity!" I said, thinking sadly of the eight young girls moving through the angular, exquisite turns and flourishes of the *gabor,* dancing for the temple or for village feasts and festivals. "Can't it be revived?"

Chokorda Rahi smiled at this example of foreign irrationality. "When Ubud people want the *gabor* again it will be revived. They became bored with the *gabor,* the girls grew up and got married, the boys began working on the Ubud *gamelan.* Now we have the best orchestra in the district."

"But no more dances?"

Chokorda Rahi looked as if he doubted my sanity. "Of course there are dances," he said, "but different ones. People in Bali get bored very easily. That is our greatest security. They constantly invent new dances and sometimes revive the old ones. But competition is fierce, so the standard must be kept high, and you can't keep high standards if people are bored." He began to name the nearby villages and their specialties. "Pliatan has an excellent *legong*, and that is the oldest Balinese dance—hundreds of years old. Blangsinga has the best *kebyar* and that is only about twenty-five years old. Sayan has a good *joget bum-bum* that was invented since you were last in Bali. But people come from everywhere to hear the Ubud *gamelan*."

The Balinese seem to have very little of what I think of as "the museum mentality," no compulsion to preserve old and beautiful things. They demand more immediate vitality from their arts. They are confident that every generation will produce beautiful new things, that it is silly to waste time keeping old ones. Temples are rebuilt every twenty or thirty years, old carvings and sculpture are casually tossed out and new ones installed. This keeps the artists and artisans busy and the people interested. On festival days Balinese women will construct the most wonderfully intricate and imaginative offerings, woven palm-leaf figures, banana-stem sculpture, lacy banners of leaves and flowers. These will be admired by the village for a few minutes, honor the gods for a few hours, and then be thrown away.

Once I asked a Balinese artist why he never signed his work. He replied seriously, "It is more difficult to write my name than to paint a picture."

"But don't you want people to know your name?"

"If a man likes my pictures I will know it. Why should he also like my name?"

"What I am trying to say is, if your pictures are good and if your name is on them, then even people who have never seen you will admire you."

"They will admire the pictures."

"Listen," I said desperately, "even after you are dead perhaps your pictures will be famous and your name will be respected. Otherwise people may forget who painted them."

He smiled with that odd Balinese assurance and, entirely missing the point, said, "Don't worry, people will not forget how to paint good pictures. After I am dead there will be many to paint good pictures."

Foreigners in Bali were appalled some time ago to see a group of young men dressed in football sweaters performing one of their classical dances. One of the boys had seen a tourist wearing such a sweater and brought the innovation back to his village. Everyone was delighted with the new look it gave to their dance, but the fad soon died out. On another occasion a Balinese girl saw a picture of an old-fashioned Russian ballerina wearing a spiky sort of crown which so charmed her that she copied it in flowers for the headdress of one of the Balinese dances. Even now, if you see a *janger,* the girls will probably be wearing the local adaptation of that Russian crown and will have forgotten, if they ever knew, its foreign origin.

That first evening in Ubud, Chokorda Agung and I walked back from our calls along Ubud's short main street—its only street. From it narrow paths lead off to smaller compounds, enclosed in mud walls and with thatched roofs to keep the rain from washing them away, and eventually to the rice fields. It was one of the few idle moments in a Balinese day. The evening cooking was done and the women sat outside their houses talking and watching the twilight settle over Ubud. The men who had been back from the fields since early afternoon and had, perhaps, played football or gone to a cockfight, now were clustered on the roadside or sat at little beer stalls drinking with their friends for a few minutes before dinner. Children ran down the street to the corner stall for a package of peanuts or a couple of clove-scented cigarettes. Everybody was back from the bathing places in the river and now looked neat with damp and glossy hair. Here and there oil lamps glowed from houses and street stalls. Now and again voices rose as a group broke up: "Safety in going. . . ." "Eat well!"

"Safety in remaining!"

There was nothing much happening around Ubud that evening—a shadow play in a village a couple of miles away, but not a particularly good troupe—and most people would go to sleep almost immediately after dinner. Only a few of the boys in the Ubud music society, who were going to a *gamelan* rehearsal, would walk home across the village green singing odd snatches of music in the dark.

I was awakened next morning just before daylight by the familiar racket of the fighting cocks crowing and fussing in their bamboo cages. They belonged, I remembered, to Chokorda Agung's cousin, a thin, shy man with the stately and charming manners of an old-fashioned Balinese. In the old days he kept fighting crickets in little bamboo tubes and fed them red peppers to make them fierce. He had a trick, during conversation, of absently releasing a cricket on his knee and gently stroking its back while he talked. He had given up his crickets, and now he concentrated on fighting cocks, which he housed in the empty pavilion of the courtyard I had been given. When I first knew him he had asked me one question about America: "Is it true that Americans keep chickens only for eating and eggs?"

"As far as I know, yes."

"What a pitiful life!" He shook his head sadly.

I lay on my hard bamboo bed staring past the whitewashed walls—bare except for one Balinese painting—to the high, shadowy peak of the thatch, and listened to the early-morning noises: a distant, almost inaudible chanting from the old Chokorda's *puri*—probably morning prayers and the recitation of the Hindu Vedas; the sharp banging of kerosene tins as the boys who fetch water for the *puri* went by to the river; a clear raised voice, a mother calling to her child. Then the sound of talk and an occasional spurt of laughter as the men started for the fields. Thus, gradually, began the mixed bustle of the new day.

As usual, the days in Ubud were full of small events and melted into the past with bewildering speed. I visited several friends and again got used to the curiously antiseptic yet very intimate "women's talk" of Bali; the immediate question, "Are you pregnant?" the clucking sympathy when I said, "No," the prompt advice to have a baby quickly before my son is three years old. I listened with fascination to the list of Ubud girls who had reached puberty and were eligible for lovemaking and marriage; and the young women who were unhappy with their husbands and what should be done about it (everything from patience to divorce, which is quite simply obtained in Bali: "no man is happy unless his wife is happy too").

Sitting informally like that in their houses, Balinese women usually wear no covering over their breasts. Or if they are working in the fields they wear no blouse because to cover your breasts in Bali is not a sign of modesty, only of wealth. If you have so many blouses that you don't mind getting them dirty in the household or field work that almost any Balinese woman does, whatever her rank, then you can extravagantly wear them all the time. Recently the government and the Balinese council of rajas, irritated by the publicity Bali's bare-breasted women had received, announced that the tourist photographs were "undignified," and that in the future Balinese women would wear blouses. Predictably enough, the Balinese didn't take much notice of this announcement and continued to dress and behave as they always had. There are two occasions when women must always cover their breasts: any visit to a temple, and any formal ceremony or social event. However, girls of marriageable age usually wear blouses. In this, as in almost everything else, the Balinese have their own rules and their own flexibility.

On those Ubud mornings, visiting the women and asking questions, the hours slipped away. We sat on the raised pavilion floors eating bananas, cubes of papaya speared on toothpicks and sweet, gelatinous rice cakes, and talking with solid realism about the common material of most people's lives.

Once I went to hear an orchestra rehearsal and was again impressed and tired from concentrating on Bali's astonishingly strong, disciplined and inventive music. One evening Chokorda Agung said that he was going to a village half an hour away to see a dance class, and would I like to go along? The teacher, he said, was famous for his skill. A couple of the boys from the Ubud orchestra decided to come with us to keep an eye on the competition and make scornful comparisons between the two *gamelans*.

After dinner we set out, carrying a couple of torches, palm fronds lashed together and soaked in coconut oil, walking at the brisk Balinese pace. Chokorda Agung explained that this village, until recently, had been too poor to afford an orchestra and dancers. In the last year, however, crops had been good and they had achieved a mild prosperity so, of course, the first thing they wanted was their own dance troupe. They had hired the teacher, an old man, who was fed and housed in the village and received a fee as well. He had picked four of the most talented village girls to learn a version of the *legong*. One of the girls gave promise of being really outstanding; the others merely seemed adequate. In Bali it doesn't seem to occur to people that anyone can't dance; everybody dances, some, of course, better than others.

Soon we turned into the paths through the rice fields, walking single file by the light of the uncertain torches. On summer nights the boys would catch fireflies and slip them inside the leader's shirt, where their flickering would give him an oddly luminous figure, easy to follow but not too glaring to spoil the enjoyment of the starlight reflected in the water, or the silhouetted palms. Occasionally Chokorda Agung burst into song, adding nonsense syllables to the *legong* music. "I am happy," he explained in the offhand Balinese way that reminds you how rarely you hear such a comment in other societies. As we passed each village we would hear the shrill barking of the dogs, and someone would call across the fields to know who we were and where we were going, soft disembodied voices in the darkness.

It was easy to tell that the village of our destination was poor. It had no rehearsal pavilion, and the troupe was using the shed where fruit, vegetables and cloth were sold on market days. The earthen floor had been swept clean and the dance area was illuminated with oil lamps while the *gamelan* played in a shifting semi-darkness at the far end. The little girls danced in their everyday clothes, with set, serious faces, eyes darting to match the hand gestures, concentrating intensely on the music and on the old teacher as he corrected the position of an elbow, or the fluid weaving of the head and neck. All around the shed the villagers crowded three and four deep, each wearing a faded *kain*, a shabby piece of cloth thrown with unstudied elegance around the head to produce that magnificent top-heavy look that is peculiarly

180

Balinese, each watching to see that their money was well spent and to take pleasure in the inevitable beauty of the dance even at a formative stage.

If I had to choose the quality that most impresses me about Bali, I suppose it would be that everyone is an artist. It is the only society I know of which accepts the creation and execution of art as a usual activity. Yet on the island there are practically no artists who are "professional." Extremely few people actually earn their livings from art. Mostly they are farmers, owners of fruit and coconut trees, of cows, pigs, chickens and always of rice fields—and the major part of their day is spent working the land. But if "amateur" implies a lower artistic level, they certainly are not amateurs, for their music, dancing, painting and sculpture can reach the highest international standards. A well-known Balinese musician once told me that anyone could learn to be an artist.

"But other countries have not found it so," I argued.

"I do not know other countries, but perhaps it is because other peoples are not free in their minds."

"Well, perhaps," I said, not entirely convinced.

"Any man can be trained to be a farmer," he told me confidently. "In the same way anyone can be trained to be an artist."

"But you need talent as well for art. Few people have that."

He kept a politely disbelieving silence, and from the Balinese evidence, I was talking nonsense.

I stayed in Ubud much longer than I had intended, but eventually I had to leave and for my last two days Chokorda Agung invited some of my favorite dancers to perform in the *puri*. One of the best *penchak* dancers lived in Ubud, and one evening he came to do the brief, dramatic dance that is accompanied only by drums and cymbals and is really a stylization of the art of self-defense. The Balinese have never fought a war and their idea of fighting has taken the form only of defense, and even then in such a remote way that it has become a dance with the flimsiest reminders of its origin. The first invasion of the island was a cultural one when Hinduism was brought to Bali by Madjapahit, the great Javanese emperor who fled with his court to Bali in the fourteenth century to escape the waves of encroaching Islam. The Moslem conversion, for some reason, skipped Bali, and the island still remains the only Hindu country outside India.

Fifty years ago when the Dutch invaded Bali, the Balinese might have been called on to fight their first war, but what actually happened is Bali's most romantically tragic story. The Dutch ships were sighted off the Balinese coast and, as they came closer, the people in the seaside villages could see the soldiers. The local raja declared that Bali must defend itself. All the young men of South Bali went to their houses and carefully dressed as they would for a very grand dance or a formal temple ceremony. They wore their gold-and-scarlet *kains*, wrapped their headbands with a special flourish, decorated themselves with the bravest of red flowers, and each carried a ceremonial dagger called a kris. They took a traditional cup of wine before they left their houses, and in a fantastic, glittering procession, marched down to the beach. There they formed themselves in long lines and each man, with a flash of the kris, took up a *penchak* pose and faced the enemy.

Apparently the Balinese believed that this would show the soldiers that Bali did not wish to be invaded, and that the Dutch would go away. With astonishment rather than fear they saw the Dutch open fire. When the first group of young Balinese in their scarlet-and-gold finery fell, and died on the sand, the rest of

182

them turned their krises on themselves rather than acknowledge such an inexplicable defeat. It was probably the most incredible mass suicide in history. Bali was conquered without more than one casualty to the Dutch.

After the *penchak* dance in Ubud, I said to Chokorda Agung, "I have been counting the hours and I have only thirty-two left in Bali. That makes me very sad."

"Well," he said briskly, "there's a good cremation over near Den Pasar tomorrow; that should cheer you up."

It proved to be a wonderful way to spend an afternoon. The bodies to be cremated had been put in a series of the most improbable effigies of cows. They were made of wood and painted in frivolous colors—pink, turquoise, yellow—and embellished with curlicues of gold. One cow was black, but even that didn't look funereal because it had gilt horns, and red and white ribbons streamed from its tail, and it was decorated with garlands of flowers. A long line of women in their finery carried offerings of flowers, food and trinkets to the cremation grounds, walking with that marvelously confident Balinese grace, backs erect, heads steady; occasionally an arm smoothly raised to adjust the palm tray of offerings on the head.

The young men of the village, in gangs of twenty and thirty, picked up the cow effigies and went whirling and galloping down the road. There was a wild, hilarious mud fight among the boys in one of the rice paddies. Three different orchestras provided music—a big, full-scale *gamelan,* a bamboo orchestra and a four-toned *angklung.* At last the effigies and their contents were burned, while the older men, dressed in checkered clothes, danced a *baris jaga* and got high on rice wine.

I returned to Ubud feeling much more cheerful. I remembered

183

the time when one of the Ubud youngsters had offered to read my palm. He held my hand open and with a grubby finger traced the letter *M* formed by the lines (most people have it). "Do you know what that *M* stands for?" he asked. "It stands for *manusia musti mati*" (mankind must die), "and that's all the fortune anyone needs to know." He rushed away laughing.

My last night in Ubud we had a big, elaborate ballet from a village about five miles away. It was held in the outer courtyard of the *puri*, where the huge gate was decorated with oil lamps that brought the carved gods and demons to flickering life. All the Ubud people had poured into Chokorda's *puri*.

The dance began, and with a kind of homesick shock I recognized the old terrifying witches of Balinese dance dramas, freezing the audience to a superstitious silence, tossing the streaming gray hair at the musicians, shaking the huge hands with their long, curled fingernails, scaring the children. It was a relief when the comic retainers came on, cavorting about to wild laughter from the children, making lewd jokes to the delight of the young men. The part I liked best was the haunting, magically beautiful dance of the *corps de ballet*, the slender, serious little girls with their precise definition of movement.

When it was all over and the crowd had disappeared, leaving the *puri* littered with dying flowers and cigarette stubs, I found Chokorda Agung to say my good-bys. I was leaving Ubud before daybreak the next morning. Smiling and indulgent, he listened to me saying, "I want to say good-by. I don't know when I shall come back. You know I shall miss all of you very much, the *puri* and Ubud—and all Bali in fact. . . ."

"Of course," Chokorda Agung replied calmly.

184

BURMA
land of laughter

AFTER OUR MONTHS IN INDONESIA, IT WAS naturally with many regrets that we decided to leave and continue our journey. We had spent longer there than in any other Southeast Asian country because it is the largest and most complex of them, and perhaps because of the length of time, we found that our son had made more friends and had slipped into the Indonesian way of life more thoroughly than he had in any other place (except Japan). In the following months we had frequent reminders from him of our Indonesian visit. At Christmastime that year he had taught his small Indonesian friends "Jingle Bells," and they politely in return had taught him a patriotic song, "*Indonesia Raya,*" which he is still apt to think of as a Christmas carol. Rice had become by far his favorite food (luckily, a preference that is easy to satisfy in Asia), and he felt that no meal—even breakfast—was really complete without it. He had learned to like his food quite highly spiced. He thought that the canned applesauce that we bought for him when we returned to Singapore was a most exotic food; however, he could recognize and state his preferences among a dozen different varieties of bananas, some that have to be cooked, some that can be eaten raw, some that should be seasoned and prepared as a vegetable, others that are treated as a dessert.

He had become so used to seeing orchids (for which Indonesia is famous) that he found them quite uninteresting, but he was charmed with a bunch of white daisies that he noticed somewhere. He could distinguish coconut palms from areca palms and both of them from the dark untidy variety from which palm beer is extracted. Whenever he felt thirsty away from home, he automatically asked for coconut water to drink. His usual greeting for friends or strangers was the Indonesian *tabe*. He had acquired a settled hatred of closed cars. After the slower pace of pedicabs, horse carts or rickshaws which have an openness that allows you to examine the countryside, the people or the shops that you pass, the dangerous speed and boring convenience of cars held no appeal to him. He had become so used to staying up late for dances or plays (snatching short naps in the dull bits) and taking a long afternoon siesta to make up, and to being accepted and quite easily accommodated wherever we might take him, that it was a long time before he grasped the idea that some adult social activities were closed to children.

When we returned to Singapore he found hotel life there both boring and puzzling (separate and early hours for children's meals, no chickens or piglets wandering into your room, everyone having to wear shoes all the time). It was with great excitement and relief that we set off for Burma. Conditions inland in northern Malaya had not improved. It was still virtually impossible to travel there, and except for the limited, carefully guarded foreign life in Penang or Kuala Lumpur, or in one or two "pacified" pockets of country, we would have been able to see and do very little in Malaya. Altogether there seemed to be no point in staying on in the oddly unsatisfying and insular life of Singapore.

Of all the countries of Southeast Asia, Burma is probably the one with the most immediate appeal. This may seem like too

extravagant a statement to those foreigners whose memories of
Burma are concerned mostly with the bitter wartime years, who
connect the place names of northern Burma with stops on
"Vinegar Joe" Stilwell's famous retreat, or who remember the
difficulties and the triumphs of the cutting of the Burma Road
through almost impenetrable jungles and mountains to link the
Chinese armies with their Western allies. Even now Rangoon
(the capital and your most likely point of arrival) is not a
startlingly beautiful city. The ride in from the airport shows only
a somewhat scrubby landscape and the usual undistinguished
suburbs. But almost at once you are aware of the special character
of the people—a blend of charm, *laissez-faire* and a lively sense
of the ridiculous.

A Burmese once remarked to me, "Burmans have really only
three basic moods—good, better and bored." Another Burman
explained, "I suppose you could call us arrogant, but we can't
make ourselves believe there is a better place to live than Burma."
(The Burmese quota for immigration to the United States is
never filled.) This attitude makes Burma refreshingly full of fun,
and her people a delight to know.

Under the Burman's good-humored tolerance of the world
about him, however, there is an occasional quick anger and a
sharp spirit of independence. The combination explodes from
time to time in sudden bursts of violence. Burmese history
hasn't been particularly calm. Sandwiched between Asia's two
largest nations, India to the west and a twelve-hundred-mile
frontier with China on the east, Burma, with only nineteen
million people, has had its share of invasions, peaceful and
military, from its neighbors. The fact that they invariably paid
tribute to Burma's appeal by giving the country complimentary
names was not much consolation. Burma has been known in its

history as "Golden Peninsula," "Golden Earth," and "Golden Land"—descriptions which cover the typical Burmese landmarks of gilded pagoda spires, the wealth of the soil and the sunny disposition of the people.

Four times in its history Burma's many small independent states and principalities have been welded together to form a free and united country: in the eleventh century (Burma's Golden Age); in the sixteenth century when Bayin Naung unified Burma; in the eighteenth century when the capital was named "Yangon" (Rangoon) or "The End of Strife"—a remarkably poor prophecy, because soon afterward Burma fought three wars with England which resulted in the country's becoming a British colony in 1885; and, a few years ago, when Burma's prime minister, U Nu, who resigned this June, quelled an insurrection and set up the present socialistic regime.

Throughout all this the Burmese sense of identity was never really shaken. You notice immediately, for instance, even on the streets of a city as westernized as Rangoon that Burmese men, more than any other Asians, wear their national dress—the *longyi*, or sarong, a short loose jacket, and a most dashing headcloth in frivolous ice-cream colors. Asian women are more conservative about their clothes, so it is not particularly surprising that you almost never see a Burmese woman in Western dress, but always in a *longyi* and white jacket fastened with fanciful buttons that may be made of diamonds and jade or glass and bone. The passion for permanent waves or the Audrey Hepburn cut that has affected most major cities in Asia has not touched the Burmese women. Their special pride is long, heavy hair beautifully arranged and decorated with flowers. Even many children wear their hair in the old-fashioned style—long on the top of the head and tied in a knot, around which the hair is clipped into a short, flopping fringe.

In their daily living, too, the Burmese stubbornly prefer their own ways—foods (including a sauce made of dried fish which foreigners find smelly, but which is necessary to any Burmese meal); entertainment (theater and dancing), and sports (boat racing). In their politicians they like a quality they call "being a Burmese Burman"—un-Westernized, that is. They tell you that their foreign service is an unpopular vocation because it involves living abroad. They remind you that Burma was one of the last British colonies and the first, since America showed the way in 1776, to gain independence.

Still, the Burmese can make fun of qualities they most admire. Ex-Prime Minister U Nu, for instance, famous for his devotion to Buddhism and his austerely simple life, was nicknamed "Not-so-Simple-Simon." The point was that his devotion and simplicity paid off by winning him the support of Burma's huge Buddhist population. Once, when I remarked to a Burmese friend on the pleasant attitude of his people, he said, "Oh, yes, we are very good at living in abject luxury." For by Asian standards Burma is rich. Its biggest economic problem is a surplus of rice.

Because the Burmese are so hospitable and so ready to share and explain their country, the traveler feels an instant closeness with Burma and its life. He makes friends and shares Burmese interests with no sense of effort. Another factor that makes social life casual is that Burmese women are independent and very far from the conventional picture of the retiring Oriental woman. Burmese women keep their maiden names even after marriage. They share equal property and inheritance rights with men, and they can divorce their husbands simply by announcing their intentions to a few respected elders. They are good businesswomen; many of them run commercial concerns and if, at first, it seems strange to see a slender Burmese woman with elegantly knotted hair and a bright silk *longyi* smoking a cigar and shrewdly discussing business, you soon accept it as another example of Burmese individuality. About one thing, however, Burmese women are most careful. Despite her equality a Burmese wife never destroys her husband's *hpon*—his maleness, or rather, as a friend explained it, "the glory or holiness of man." She is always respectful, and she is careful to avoid putting her *longyi* on his bed or touching his possessions with her feet.

Much impressed by the foreigners' enthusiasm for Burma and the Burmese, and wondering if the Burmese saw themselves in the same rosy light, I once asked a friend what she thought were the most obvious faults of the Burmese character. She replied, after some thought, "We don't realize the value of hard work. We have no sense of time. And we make no effort to make people like us." Confusingly enough, in the last few years a great deal has been accomplished in the country, and besides, Burma has gained considerably in international stature. While Burmans haven't learned a sense of time, foreigners soon discover that unconcern with time appears to disrupt their lives very little. Finally, of course, everyone likes the Burmese very much anyway.

Even in politics the magic seems to work. A Burmese journalist once said to me: "Although Burma's foreign policy is almost exactly the same as India's, if India's prime minister argues for coexistence the Western press criticizes him hotly. But if our prime minister does the same, everyone says, 'We perfectly understand the difficulties of your position.' Can you explain it?"

I never did find a satisfactory explanation, but, like everyone else, I too left Burma ready to sympathize with almost anything.

Next to the appeal of the Burmese people, your strongest impression of Burma is likely to be of a deeply felt, if casually observed, religion. It is probably the most intensely Buddhist country in the world. The two indispensable features of any Burmese scene are the tapering, gilt peaks of pagodas and the saffron robes of priests. Even in Rangoon, a busy, crowded modern port, architecturally an unfortunate mixture of public buildings in a "British colonial" style (onion domes, meaningless towers, weirdly ornate arcades and cornices) and the concrete cubes of offices and new apartment buildings, the whole city is given character by the dominating spire of the Shwedagon Pagoda, while the smaller Sule Pagoda marks the exact center of town.

Any morning on Rangoon's streets you will see the groups of shaven-headed priests, monks and acolytes standing before shops and houses, their begging bowls held before them, waiting for whatever food (vegetarian) the devout townspeople may give them. Every Burman in his youth enters a monastery as a novice. He may stay only a few weeks, or for years, or even dedicate his entire life to religion. He may go only to learn to read and write, or to study the fundamentals of Buddhism, or to acquire his full education. But he is sent there by his mother with the traditional request that he be beaten if he is bad. (Burmese mothers are too affectionate to beat their sons.) And he leaves the monastery with a respect for his religion and a familiarity with its principles that last him all his life.

Even with this rigorous background, there is little that is forbidding to a Burman in his religion. He will take off his shoes before he enters a pagoda, but no further deference is expected of him. In the immense, circular Shwedagon, Burma's most famous place of worship and the world's largest Buddhist pagoda, the Burmese patter briskly up the four huge stairways. They stop to greet friends, pausing at one of the stalls to buy flowers for offerings. At another stall, they bargain for toys for their children—gay and imaginative wooden animals, comical puppets, painted umbrellas. Perhaps they buy a small lacquer figure of Buddha to send to some unfortunate provincial cousins who have no chance to visit the sacred Shwedagon. Almost certainly they stop for a cup of coffee, sweets for the children or a coconut to offer at a shrine. These long entrance passages have the air of a thriving bazaar.

Even on the high main terrace, where all the many shrines are built and where Buddha statues tower in alcoves or huddle in tiny niches, the atmosphere remains casual and friendly. Children slide about on the tiles, kicking aside the withering flowers from past devotions; women wander by carrying their bundles, talking intimately as though they were going marketing; men who may be prostrating themselves will pause to stare at a stranger. But, also, there will be a mystic, so lost in meditation that no expression alters his face as he sits cross-legged in a corner, no muscle moves when people gaze at him, there is no hint of weariness or distraction to relieve his rigid pose.

From somewhere comes the chanting of scriptures punctuated by the sharp resonance of a bell; priests and devout laymen are saying prayers among the twinkling crystals, the mirrored shrines, the lacy, gilded decorations of the pavilions. Rising high into the pale Burmese sky above the worshipers is the golden spire of the Shwedagon.

The Burmese, with their natural sense of enjoyment, make their religious festivals among the most entertaining in the world. Except during the Buddhist Lent (usually July through September) there is a festival of some sort almost every fortnight. There are big festivals at both the beginning and end of Lent, when all Burma is decorated with lights and for three days there are feasts and almsgiving.

New Year's (which comes in mid-April) is celebrated with a water festival, when the images of Buddha are ritually washed in perfume; the children have converted the solemn business of being blessed with holy water into a water fight.

Then there is the fire festival of mid-November, and festivals for the various important stages in the life of Buddha. And besides all these, every full moon deserves a celebration, and every pagoda has its own annual festival, and every family has its special ceremonies when a boy shaves his head to enter a monastery, or when a girl has the lobes of her ears pierced.

Next to Japan, Burma is more theatrically-minded than any other nation in Asia, and their *pwes* (a word which covers everything from historical drama to musical comedy) always seem to be packed with people who are happy to sit all night on reed mats watching a biographical play about an ancient Burmese king or a variety show with dozens of changes of scene and costume. You may be invited to go to the theater at midnight or at three in the morning—your host may have been watching the show since nine at night, but since foreigners don't have such stamina, he may, politely, have asked you only for the most interesting part or for the moment when the lead dancer appears. In any case, you will see a profoundly Burmese art and entertainment.

Unless it is one of the rare modern plays, music and the dance will undoubtedly be mixed in with straight theater. The Burmese orchestra—one of the most decorative I have seen—is set a little below the level of the stage.

The *saing-waing*, the most important instrument, looks like a fantastic mirrored and gilded circular cage. Inside are a series of graded drums, each tuned with a blob of rice paste in the middle, and in the center the musician sits on a tiny stool, swinging from side to side, beating the drums, setting the mood and the pace for the orchestra.

Around this leader are ranged the flute and drum players, and on one side, slung from a fabulous golden frame, are the two huge gongs that maintain the basic beat of the music. The dancers appear, dressed in the most luxurious of *longyis,* jackets and jewelry, and face the audience with almost formidable assurance. They joke and flirt with men in the orchestra, and then, suddenly, they flare into short bursts of dancing, as brilliant and surprising as firecrackers.

Immediately after a famous dancer has been wildly applauded, a comedian may do an absurd take-off on the same dance, and his casual ridicule of a great art form draws equally enthusiastic appreciation.

Though Buddhism plays so large a part in the life, entertainment and character of the Burmese, at the same time they prudently keep on good terms with the *nats*—vaguely defined as spirits of inanimate (and sometimes animate) things. You may meet a Burman who seems in every way sophisticated, realistic, even cynical. As you get to know him better you may discover that he never takes a journey without first checking with an astrologer, or never sets the date for an important family event— a daughter's wedding, or a move to a new home—without first determining the most auspicious day and hour. In the case of a new house, he would first hang coconuts from its eaves to keep the evil *nats* out. Even the former prime minister, they tell you, once returned a defective radio with the comment that his house *nats* didn't like it.

Outside a Buddhist pagoda there is often another shrine for the *nats* so they won't be jealous; and in the spring, when for some

196

reason the *nats* most need to be pacified, all over Rangoon there are *nat* dances and offerings.

When you see a *nat* dance, you realize it is a trance dance. The woman dancer sits on the ground in front of a shelf piled with offerings. As the orchestra plays loudly, she gets up smiling quite ordinarily and begins her dance. Somewhere in the course of it the *nats* take over and give her a new personality. She may become, for instance, a little girl with a pettish expression, childish gestures and the inexpert, touching movements of a child learning to dance; she will seem to be bouncing a ball, tying ribbons in her hair, playing with her friends. Or she may become a drunkard, reeling clumsily about, belligerently pushing away friends who try to restrain her.

One *nat* dancer I saw became the soul of generosity—she gave away everything she possessed to people in the audience or the orchestra. At the end I found myself, considerably embarrassed, holding a bunch of bananas, three eggs, an orange and a four-yard length of silk. The finish of the dance is marked by an uncontrollable shaking as the *nat* leaves the dancer's body.

To anyone who knows Mandalay only sentimentally from Kipling's poem, it comes as a dispiriting lesson in geography to learn that Mandalay is nowhere near the sea, there are no flying fish (even the Irrawaddy River, Burma's great waterway, is a couple of miles away and you can't even see it from the city unless you climb to the top of Mandalay Hill) and the dawn comes up quite prosaically from across a wide and dusty plain. However, Mandalay is, in every other sense, a magnificent place, and, as the Burmese are sure to tell you, "it is the indestructible heart of Burma."

Even from the plane, as you approach the Mandalay airfield,

you see the city's unmistakable profile: the slender peaks—white-washed, gilded or mud-colored—of hundreds of pagodas, stupas and shrines. On the streets there are constant reminders of Mandalay's intense Buddhism. Signs in shop windows and on walls ask you to "Be Kind to Animals by Not Eating Them."

Surprisingly, Mandalay is, in Asian terms, a new city, less than a hundred years old. It has been extensively battered in the last fifteen years, first by the invading Japanese, then by the returning Allies and most recently by Burma's own insurgents. But it occupies a very special emotional and artistic position in Burmese history. It was founded as a royal capital by unanimous decision of the court astrologers and necromancers, and the last of the Burmese monarchs, King Thibaw, ruled here. At the same time, it was established as a religious center, and even now some of Burma's most respected holy men and mystics preach and meditate in its pagodas and monasteries. Finally, it is Burma's cultural capital and everywhere there are echoes of the past.

Southwest of Mandalay is one of Southeast Asia's richest archaeological treasure houses—the ancient, eleventh-century capital of Pagan, "the city of five thousand pagodas." At its height it was one of the wonders of the continent, the heart of a rich and peaceful empire until Kublai Khan invaded Pagan and left it to disintegrate in the dusty plain of the Irrawaddy. Deserted now, Pagan and its sixteen square miles of ruins, dominated by the graceful towers and magnificent arcades of the great Ananda pagoda, still holds, almost as strongly as Angkor, that impressive, haunting atmosphere of the lost great past of Southeast Asia.

Mandalay has a livelier and more insouciant air. If you climb the thousand steps to the top of Mandalay Hill, on the edge of the city, you look down into the old palace grounds, two square miles enclosed in massive crenelated walls and further protected by a moat, and imagine the splendid life of Mandalay under the Burmese kings. Before World War II the red and black lacquered pillars of the palace were famous, and the huge curving roofs glittered silver in the sun. Now, only the platforms of the pavilions remain and fragments of the arcades among the shady gardens where the queens used to play hide-and-seek with their ladies in waiting. Around the palace stretch the crowded city streets, broken here and there by the many pagodas.

The acknowledged gem of all of them is the Golden Monastery, a fantasy of gilded wooden lace, carved in dizzying detail to form the walls, balustrades, pillars, eaves and ceilings of a small shrine set outside the Incomparable Pagoda. At the foot of Mandalay Hill is the "Pagoda of the Scriptures," simpler, more austere in style; here if you drop a coin into the contribution box, the old guardian will ring his bell to call the attention of the spirits and chant a prayer for you.

Mandalay Hill itself is encrusted with pagodas, shrines, monasteries and eating places, all clinging to its steep sides like limpets to a rock. Each has its particular attraction. In one there is a wishing stone which you lift once, with both hands, then make your wish and lift again. If it seems heavier the second time, your wish will come true.

An extraordinary sight at any time, Mandalay Hill is best seen during a festival when the long stairways become saffron ribbons as thousands of monks climb the hill to make their devotions, and there is an incessant tinkling of tiny wind bells that decorate every shrine. But even on ordinary nights the sight of Mandalay Hill, a sharp illuminated cone shining green against the black sky, is the city's favorite, most characteristic landmark.

Modernization comes only slowly to Mandalay—the usual conveyance, for instance, is still the old-fashioned hansom cab, implacably Victorian in appearance, but lightened with bells and garlands on the horses and sometimes garishly painted. Should you see a *shinpyu* procession leaving a house after the head-shaving ceremony for a small boy, it will be arranged in the correct old manner, the boy riding on a decorated pony (or, in richer families, a cart), the relatives and friends dressed in the costume of ministers of the court, the priests, yellow robed as always, and everything accompanied by the beating of gongs and cymbals.

Even if the rest of Burma becomes slowly westernized, even if, as a Mandalay acquaintance said, "In Rangoon they begin to drink whisky-soda and spend their evenings in a club," the old manners and traditions and arts will at least be maintained in Mandalay.

From Mandalay eastward begins the great Shan plateau, sheltered to the north from Tibet by a gigantic horseshoe of mountains where dozens of different groups of hill people live —the Chins, Kachins, Nagas, Lolos, to mention only a few.

The best way to visit the northern Shan States from Mandalay is by car. You can hire a jeep to take you up the alarming (but quite safe) road that climbs eastward to the hill resort of May-myo, where even in February you will find delicious strawberries sold on the roadside by Gurkha tribesmen (eight big baskets for a dollar), roses in the gardens and, most precious of all, what the Burmese call "two-blanket weather." Beyond Maymyo, the road dips perilously down hillsides, spans ravines on slender bridges, climbs past the northern Shan capital of Lashio to the jade-green mountains and incredible vistas of the Chinese borderlands. On your way you spend your nights in government "Travelers'

Bungalows," and your days exploring villages or tea plantations, and in the dry winter season there is nearly always a *pwe* somewhere in the vicinity.

From the lookout pavilion on the border you can stare into the rocky, improbably dramatic gorges of China itself, resembling the most stylized of Chinese paintings. To those whose knowledge of Burma is associated with wartime memories of the bitter jungle fighting in these hills, the winding track has a different significance—this was the western end of the vital Burma Road.

If you are a bit more adventurous, you can follow the China frontier to the town of Namkam (headquarters of Dr. Seagrave, author of *Burma Surgeon*) and from there continue to Bhamo, the country of the Chins and Kachins who still tattoo themselves from thigh to waist in fantastic designs. Their tattoos are a matter of great pride. In one dance I witnessed, a Chin boy was the only one who stubbornly insisted on dancing in long trousers. The others wore tight loincloths. When the dance leader told him to roll up his trouser legs for the sake of symmetry, he shamefacedly explained, "I haven't yet been able to get my thighs tattooed."

From Bhamo you can take the magnificent three-day boat journey down the Irrawaddy to Mandalay. In the Shan States southeast of Mandalay is Taunggyi, capital of the whole Shan plateau, an untidy-looking town, casually scattered about the side of a hill. If its architecture is undistinctive, its gardens and flowering trees are theatrically lavish. The town and the surrounding hillsides are covered in exuberant succession all through the winter with pale clouds of cherry blossoms, the unearthly blue of jacaranda, white bouhenia (its flowers are used in cooking a fragrant stew), poinsettia (both the color of parchment and the more familiar scarlet), flame of the forest, the sharp in-

201

credible pink of cassia, and a tree I never identified whose bark is said to be an antidote to drunkenness. Altogether they give Taunggyi a light-opera air, intensified by the friendliness of almost any Shan you meet.

If your visit coincides with one of the "five-day markets" (held every five days, not lasting five days), Taunggyi will offer an exciting glimpse of the people and handicrafts of the Shan countryside. For on market day the people come down from their mountain villages, the members of each tribe in their distinctive costumes and jewelry, to exchange their finely woven cloth and their capacious, decorative shoulder bags for salt, staples and town goods. You will see beautifully carved and etched silver work as well as the wonderful lacquerware for which Burma is famous.

About an hour's drive from Taunggyi is the strangely lovely country around Lake Inle, home of the Inthas. To reach the lake, you hire a boat in the nearest village and follow a narrow channel cut through the marshes. Winding among the high reeds, you feel curiously adventurous, isolated and somehow ominous, like a scene from the *African Queen*. Here and there along the channel are gingerbread pergolas with lotuses carved on their eaves; beyond the reeds stretch the paddy fields with always a flight of white herons swinging down in sleek lines to settle on the young rice.

Suddenly from the narrow tunnel you come out into the open lake, a calm, pastel, misty expanse of water, like a painting on silk. All around are tiny green islands, and between them the slender Intha boats flit to the fish traps, the duck-shooting marshes and the villages on the far shore. The boats are hollowed-out teak trees, which are propelled by the most extraordinary rowing technique I have seen. The Intha oarsman stands at the back of the shell, a leg wrapped around the oar, and with a backward kick he forces the oar through the water.

The lake people have a peculiarly gentle nature and so great an affection for their shallow, beautiful lake that they are said to grow thin from misery if they ever leave it. There is no robbery among them, so the story goes, and no bandits, even though parts of northern Burma are still plagued by that hangover of wartime, guerrillas. The Inthas live entirely off their lake, even raising vegetables on floating gardens. In the middle of the lake there is a most surprising and pleasing resthouse, built on stilts, where you can spend the night or stop for a meal.

On the far side of Inle are weaving villages whose women produce intricate designs in clear primary colors that are typical of the Shan peoples. The largest of the lake villages, Ywama, has the enchantment that goes with places that make only a casual distinction between water and land. Most of the houses are built on stilts over the water. The twelve monasteries with their towers and domes throw crinkled reflections on the village's main thoroughfare, a wide, half-tamed strip of the lake. There Ywama's daily market is held, and boats from neighboring villages come skimming in loaded with fish, fruit and vegetables.

In smaller boats the women come to market and, with expert flicks of their paddles, weave between the merchants' boats, fingering a piece of cloth, poking vegetables to see if they are fresh, piling their purchases in their boats. Friends will call to each other, and sidle their boats to the channel edge to gossip. Before they return home they may stop at the restaurant boat for a snack or a cup of coffee.

With all these diversities of country, populations and cultures, postwar Burma was presented with some of the most formidable problems of any Southeast Asian country. Its towns and countryside had been ravaged by the war, it had been the battlefield for two huge armies. It then had to come to grips with a nation-wide Communist-led insurrection. Three things, the Burmese feel, saved their country: the pacific and unifying power of Buddhism, the determination of their prime minister, U Nu, and the fact that a Burman refuses to be bullied. To which a foreigner is inclined to add a fourth: the Burmese independent and down-to-earth character. The astonishing and admirable results have been that within a few years the many states and tribes have become a more or less unified country, internal Communism is no longer a threat, and a free and democratic government is getting ahead with the work of building a welfare state. But the endearing thing about the Burmese is that through all this they have retained their sobriquet of "the Land of Laughter."

On one occasion, when I went to a *pwe* with some Burmese friends, some of us got sleepy before the end of the performance (it was then four in the morning). On the way home I asked my host to tell me the end of the story. Did the tangled romance end in separation, death and tragedy? Or were the lovers reunited and the obstacles overcome?

"Don't you know?" he said, laughing. "All Burmese stories have happy endings."

CEYLON
tropic island paradise

CEYLON, THAT PEAR-SHAPED ISLAND SET BE-
tween the south of India and the Equator, is the only country
of Southeast Asia that was virtually untouched by the last World
War. It had, in the last thousand years of its history, known four
different colonial rulers (more than any other nation in Asia),
but at least it escaped the occupation of the Japanese that spread
with such alarming speed through the rest of the region. Of
course, it was used as a naval base during the war, and saw its
share of the ebb and flow of troops through the island, and
it was, besides, Lord Louis Mountbatten's headquarters for a
large part of the Southeast Asian campaign. However, in spite
of colonizations, Ceylon has had a more untroubled history than
its Asian neighbors. Its character is far less thorny than that of
India, immediately to the north, its country far less ravaged
or dislocated than Burma, Malaya or Indonesia. It has always
seemed able to absorb, with a curiously unruffled ease, the many
foreign influences that have come its way, and usually, through
its beauty or natural courtesy, it has left an equally indelible
mark on its visitors or conquerors. One ancient writer seeing
Ceylon for the first time compared it to a garden filled with "the
joy of spring . . . resplendent with fair dwellings . . . an elixir
to the eyes. . . ."

More recent visitors have had something of the same feeling
about it and Ceylon has been for years a favorite place with

foreigners who, having spent most of their working lives in Asia, when the moment comes for them to retire cannot imagine returning to the more austere and expensive life of their home countries. They particularly like to settle in the cool, misty mountains of central Ceylon, around the resort town of Nuwara Eliya, where the hillsides are terraced with immense tea gardens, where the shooting is good, the walks are beautiful, providing some of the most impressive scenery in Southeast Asia, and the social life is geared to the leisurely pace and pleasant neighborliness of the plantations.

Altogether (always with the exception of Bali, though that is perhaps a private preference) Ceylon is better organized for tourism than any other country in Southeast Asia. Accommodations are always adequate and sometimes excellent—the island has a convenient system of government-owned and run "resthouses" in every famous beauty spot, near all the sites of historic or artistic interest, and provides for the holiday traveler a wide variety of pleasures and activities, ranging from the simple business of loafing on a perfect beach to the more specialized amusements of classical dance or archaeological inquiry. Partly because of the fortuitous pattern of history that has given Ceylon a relative calm in recent years, and partly because of the look and nature of the island and the people that live in it, Ceylon is probably the most rewarding part of Southeast Asia for casual travel.

You arrive at the Ratmalana airport, eight miles out of Colombo, Ceylon's capital, and drive south. Just outside the airport you may see some of Ceylon's famous elephants, mostly dark gray but becomingly mottled about the ears and trunk with pink, plodding down the road with their young mahouts perched on their necks or carrying home a meal of enormous palm fronds. As soon as you leave the glum suburbs of the crowded capital, the road turns and dips with the coastline, never more than yards from the ocean, and all the way south to Galle or Matara you follow a shore scalloped with beaches, shaded by coconut and breadfruit trees. Here and there a cluster of azure-washed houses and thatched shacks forms a village; little gray monkeys scurry out of the road as you pass; sometimes you glimpse a child solemnly guiding a giant iguana on a leash, women pounding rice, a painted oxcart, a group of young men in checked sarongs or girls dressed in the favorite Ceylon colors—clear aquamarine and hot pink. And beyond the trees and huts, close to the slender fishing boats drawn up on the sand, you are always conscious of the glittering blue or green or milky celadon of the Ceylon sea. It is almost too classically correct a landscape, almost too lovely; but you can no more help being captivated first by Ceylon's beauty, then by its people and its life, than could all the others who have come here through the centuries as traders, conquerors or travelers.

Greeks, Moors, Tamils, Portuguese, Dutch; each in turn gave the island some of the most heady and evocative names in history —Taprobane, Tenerisim, Ilanare, Hibenard, Serendib; and left behind a string of dizzy sobriquets as well—"Isle of Spices," "Pearl of the Indian Ocean," "Isle of Delight." All this doesn't seem too outrageously fulsome when you are in Ceylon itself, and even the Sinhalese who might, through familiarity, have become offhand about their countryside, are continually taking bus trips to famous beauty spots, visiting historic monuments, going up to the mountains or down to the coast, or wandering through the rich and exciting game reserves. Recently, sitting on the sea wall of the small southern town of Weligama, I remarked to a Sinhalese friend that I had been much impressed by the easy Sinhalese acceptance of foreigners, that even after four long and rigid colonizations there seemed to be virtually no bitterness or suspicion.

"But to us," my friend replied, "it seems easy to understand. When you look at something like this"—he waved his hand at the sapphire water and curving yellow beaches of Weligama Bay —"you realize at once that any foreigner seeing it would want to own it. Particularly," he added with a touch of condescension, "a European." For a moment I, too, felt almost sorry for those poor pale Europeans surrounded by their gray and chilly northern waters. Unlike other Asian countries eager to assert their new independence from colonial rulers, Ceylon feels no comparable nationalistic urgency. It remained until last year, by choice, within the British Empire, allowed England to take care of any defense requirements, and accepted Queen Elizabeth II as sovereign of Ceylon.

This pleasant and generous nature of the Sinhalese is a quality you come to value as highly as the beauty of the island, the fire of Sinhalese dancing, the pageantry of its festivals or the crumbling magnificence of its ancient cities. Any number of times, when I stopped in a small village to ask for something to drink, a small boy was immediately sent shinning up a coconut tree for a green coconut (or occasionally the sweet Sinhalese specialty, a golden king coconut) filled with cloudy coconut water. Once, when I stopped to stare at the colored lights and decorations outside a village house—in honor of a wedding—the parents of the bride came out and invited me to join the wedding party. Another time, when an American friend and I paused to watch a dance being held outside a home, the host called us into the shelter of the canopy where the family sat, found us chairs, and summoned a man who knew English to explain the story and the movements of the dance. Such courtesies are the ordinary currency of social exchange in Ceylon.

Probably the best way to see Ceylon is by car; the roads are good, cars are easy and reasonable to hire in Colombo, and distances are short. Besides, the island has an excellent system of government resthouses where travelers can stop for a meal, a night or a weekend, and many of the most entrancing places can be reached only by road. Look at a map of Ceylon and you will find that dozens of towns, even modern ones, have retained the intoxicating names associated with remote pirates and priva- teers and clipper ships trading long ago in spices and gems and tea. Trincomalee, for instance, or Jaffna, Negombo, Kandy—all turn out to be as attractive as their names—but the astonishing thing is that in so compact an island they should also provide such sharp differences of country and atmosphere. Jaffna, for example, is an old Dutch town in the far north of the island, surrounded by vast salt flats, and famed for some of its more peculiar exports—turtles and sea slugs (for Chinese cooking), mangoes and tobacco and a special kind of mollusk used in making shell jewelry. To reach Jaffna you must drive through the wide, dry plains of the north until you come to the shallow inlet of Elephant Pass, where the huge animals, originally forced south from the Indian mainland, forded the straits to take sanctu- ary in Ceylon. Trincomalee, on the rich east coast with its fine harbors, cliffs, deep-sea fishing and its humid jungles, is a port town that dominates the great China Bay and its treacherous outer boundary, Foul Point. Here, the Sinhalese tell you, are Ceylon's best sailors, and its people have the reputation of being direct, a little stern, and very industrious. But in Negombo, in the heart of the lush west-coast country, the people are easy-going and pleasure-loving; small boats skim across its lagoons and you are served at least three kinds of fish at each meal.

Yet Kandy, in the cool green mountains of central Ceylon, only a couple of hours away by car, is completely distant in character. It is a lovely summer resort that mixes a holiday atmosphere with a deep sense of its own history and elegance. For Kandy is a city that held out against all invaders and colonizers for centuries and was finally ceded to the British scarcely more than a century ago, and it has a special pride in its independent traditions. As the capital of the last dynastic rulers of Ceylon, the Kandyan kings, it claimed the highest aristocracy—even today there are Sinhalese ladies here who prefer not to receive people with the common local names of De Silva or Fernandez or the like, because a name of such obvious Portuguese origin can only mean that the family was of very poor standing in the sixteenth century when the Portuguese first captured parts of Ceylon, and consequently permitted marriages with foreigners. Besides this rarefied concern with good breeding, they are among the few people in Ceylon who fret about the island's rapidly disintegrating caste system and draw fine social distinctions between the highest land-owning caste and the lesser fisher castes or drummer castes.

Equally, however, Kandy is famous as a cultural center (much strengthened by the great university town of Peradeniya only four miles away), known for its writers, scholars, artists and musicians. Its dancers are the most famous in Ceylon today, and have over the centuries evolved Ceylon's best-known form of dancing. The Kandyan dancers in their white-and-silver costumes, each with a spiderweb of beads stretched across the chest, are an essential part of every festival, of every big party; they leap and whirl through the streets in every major procession,

212

and have spread their high exuberance and deep intensity through all Sinhalese dancing.

The resort-town aspects of Kandy are perhaps more immediately apparent, in the casual atmosphere and the unexacting pleasures of the town. Any evening, about an hour before sunset, you can watch the elephants bathing in the river after their work in the fields and forests. With absurd and ponderous gaiety they sluice water over each other and wallow in the shallows near the riverbank, and stagger out to plod home through the city streets. Or you can have a program of Kandyan dances performed for you for ten dollars, though if you want the greatest of the dancers, a charming and unassuming old man called Gunaya, it will cost about twice as much. Or, for less theatrical taste, there are walks and shoots in the beautiful hills around the town, shopping for Kandy's antique silverware and lacquerwork, parties in the hillside bungalows, and weekends spent on the chilly heights of the tea plantations in the mountains.

Yet another attraction in Kandy is the Temple of the Sacred Tooth of Buddha, Buddhist Ceylon's most revered place of worship. The shrine itself is an unpretentious octagonal building jutting out from a beautiful entranceway of carved arches and shallow steps banked with the displays of flower vendors and constantly illumined by the golden robes of the Buddhist priests. Inside the outer hall there are bright frescoes of moments in the life of Buddha as well as more lurid depictions of the torments of sinners; and finally the Tooth itself, enclosed in six inner shrines all gilded and set with precious stones.

Ceylon's splashiest festival and wildest celebration takes place in Kandy every August, at the time of the full moon, when the Sacred Tooth is carried in procession through the city. Thousands

213

of people from all over Ceylon crowd into the city to see the immense and lavish *perahera*—a cavalcade of priests and laymen, chieftains in all their jeweled finery, fabulously caparisoned elephants, of standard-bearers and drummers, and, inevitably, of groups of Kandyan dancers—all led by the traditional whip wielders who plunge down the roads scaring away demons.

Ceylon's form of Buddhism is much less demonstrative than the later forms found in other parts of Asia—except for such gaudy festivals as the Kandy *perahera*, or the Sinhalese New Year, which arrives in April after the big harvest. (On this occasion astrologers, in whom the Sinhalese have considerable faith, determine auspicious colors for people to wear and the correct moment of the day to anoint themselves with oil or to eat the first meal of the year.) Wesak, in May, which commemorates Buddha's birth, enlightenment and death, and calls for elaborate decoration and illumination of every home, is also a splashy day of celebration. Compared with the golden pagodas of Burma, or the fantasies of carving, gilt and crockery that decorate the temples of Thailand, Ceylon's most sacred Buddhist monuments are simple to a point of extreme austerity. Whitewash is considered the only suitable adornment for the most famous of the island's stupas—the great Ruanwelli of Anuradhapura—and in many shrines the sole decorations are flower offerings left by devotees.

Ceylon was among the first of the Asian countries to adopt Buddhism as its national religion. In 307 B.C. the son of the great Indian emperor Asoka came to the island as a Buddhist missionary to preach a new religion that was so simple and exacting that not even an image of the Buddha was permitted in its places of worship. Later generations softened some of the rules, but for two thousand years Buddhism has remained the religion of Ceylon; and for twelve centuries, with only one break, the religious center was Anuradhapura, capital of the ancient Sinhalese kings.

Today, Anuradhapura, a somewhat haphazard town with new buildings mixed in with the ruined mounds and monuments, still carries deep religious authority in the Buddhist world; you can see the vast severe domes that date from the third century B.C. (though the largest is depressingly surrounded by a modern concrete frieze of elephant heads), you can speculate about the little groves of chiseled granite pillars that jut at crazy angles here and there among the buildings, or you can, rather pleasantly, acquire merit by visiting the sacred Bo Tree, brought here by the daughter of the Emperor Asoka and for ten cents have it watered by a special sprinkler system.

Probably the most stimulating of the island's great historic sights is the ruined city of Polonnaruwa, a magnificent cluster of palaces, shrines and carvings set by an extraordinarily lovely lake. One of its most impressive monuments is an enormous rock face carved with three gigantic figures: a meditating Buddha, the statue of a disciple, and, most famous of all, the Sleeping Buddha.

A short distance away are the ruins of the Sacred Quadrangle, on the edge of the lake, among shade trees and flower gardens, and filled with fantasy and charm. Here among the ruins is the flowery little pavilion from which a twelfth-century king "listened to the chanting of 'protective texts' "; nearby is a huge stone book, carved like the old papyrus documents, which records the king's great deeds. A tall statue of Buddha stands isolated among the flowers, the shrine which surrounded him entirely disintegrated. A wonderfully elaborate "Embellished Stupa" (strangely frivolous compared with earlier Buddhist structures), partly ruined, still displays its beautiful circular colonnades, an exuberance of carving, and the most beautiful of the semicircular thresholds enchantingly decorated with elephants, lions and ducks, that are known and admired all through Ceylon as "Moonstones."

The most celebrated single monument in Polonnaruwa is a huge standing figure of Buddha called the Lankatilleke, the Jewel of Ceylon, at one time the masterwork of all Buddhist Asia; but my own favorite among the dozens of ruins is the rose-pink Tivanka shrine. Its roof crumbled away long ago, so that now you see the headless standing Buddha, severely elegant of line but softened by the warm color of the stone, in the uncompromising relief of direct sunlight against the deep blue of Ceylon's sky. On the walls of the narrow hall that leads to the Tivanka statue are some of the most charming frescoes in Asia. The colors have dimmed to a subtle range of russets, sepias and tans, but fugitive scenes of wasp-waisted court ladies, or occasionally the seductive pose of a dancer, can still be seen, with here and there only the exquisite lines of a face or a hand. It is a small shrine, set on a slight hill. A few yards away the tangled jungle begins, alive with the quarrelsome chatter of monkeys.

The most dramatic of Ceylon's ancient cities is Sigiriya, the "Fortress in the Sky," a weird monument built on an immense outcropping of granite rising four hundred feet sheer out of the northern plain. Here a wicked king of the fifth century buried his father alive in a wall, and then, half demented by fear, he erected "an impregnable, twisted city of steps." On one crag he built a massive lion's head; on different platforms he constructed baths and reservoirs. Wide galleries on which four men could walk abreast, terraces, an audience hall, and even elephant stalls were laboriously chiseled out of the granite. On this extraordinary rock, according to one account, he lived eighteen years of terror, "surrounding himself with lissome, voluptuous women and living a riotous life, trying to forget his aching conscience and the gnawing remorse in his heart." If you are reasonably athletic, you can climb the stairway that rises in dizzying grades and see the portraits of the seminude women of that fantastic court painted on the walls of one of the galleries; you can climb still higher to the feet of the rock lion and the fragments of the old palace.

Unimaginably remote in feeling from these legacies of Ceylon's past are the island's modern cities. You are almost certain to arrive in Colombo, the capital, the chief port and only commercial air field. You will find a modern city, something over fifty years old, with some good hotels, clubs, shops and movies, with a hectic bazaar district (known by the old colonial types as "the native quarter," but by the Sinhalese as the "Petah"). But you will also find that confusing muddle of architecture, none of it very good, consisting of Doric pillars on the town hall, a "Saracenic" style for the Eye Hospital, Muslim minarets, and Dutch colonial houses, which has given a peculiar and disturbing character to many modern Asian towns.

Far more pleasing, to me at least, is the old port of Galle on the lovely southern coast. Although less bustling than Colombo, more predictable in its countryside than the hill resorts, without the historical treasures of ancient Sinhalese architecture and sculpture, it is by far the most appealing town on the island for its easygoing atmosphere, the slightly inquisitive but always friendly approach of its people, its gently decaying reminders of the old colonial life mixed with a more vigorous Sinhalese activity in the newer sections of Galle.

Someone once described Galle to me as the place where

"the fish in the market are the color of rubies and you can buy cinnamon stick by the yard"—both facts are true, and in a way they are typical of the odd concentration of romance and practicality in the city. The old section of the town is built on a narrow spit of land enclosed in the massive walls and fortifications that date from the eras of the Portuguese and Dutch rule, though now, of course, they serve only to give Galle that special charm that seems to belong to any walled city. Nowadays goats and children skip up the old turrets and one often sees, silhouetted against the sky and sea, the bizarre sight of a cow strolling precariously on the battlements searching for the tufts of grass that grow between the crenelations. Among the narrow streets and old mansions of the fort it is easy to imagine the strange and rigid life that the Dutch rulers of the eighteenth century brought to Galle at a time when it was the most important harbor of Ceylon (Colombo was scarcely a village), and its bay was filled with huge clipper ships, the famous Indiamen and the coastal paddleboats.

On the steps before the beautiful façade of the old Dutch church the prominent families must have gathered on Sundays, and today you can still see the memorial tablets and coats-of-arms of the people that lived and died there. You will probably stay in the hotel next to the church, converted from an old private residence (and rather incongruously called the New Oriental Hotel), where you will find exactly the kind of spacious high-ceilinged comfort that you expect, old-fashioned, and very much in keeping with the Galle atmosphere. In the governor's residence just down the road, the great balls were held; on the verandahs of the old houses the Dutch ladies entertained their friends to tea, screened from the road by *tats*—decorative reed or wooden lattices stretched between the verandah pillars at eye

level. Even now people in Galle will tell you of the touchy arrogance of those Dutch settlers whose ghosts are everywhere in
the fort—how one of the early governors wore a patch over one
eye for no reason except to show the Sinhalese that he didn't
need two eyes to rule so small a colony, or how the Dutch ladies
once refused to attend a governor's ball in honor of an Englishman because they were so offended by a recent English publica-
tion that made the comment, "The Dutch ladies have a custom
of cracking their joints, and rubbing them over with oil, which
renders them uncommonly supple."

If you walk down the twisting roads of the fort you are in a
delightful but slightly Alice-in-Wonderland sort of world. You
find yourself in a perfect miniature plaza, scarcely changed in
three hundred years, but close by a space has been cleared for a
whitewashed stupa incongruous in its setting of gray battlements.
You walk through a magnificent arch cut through a fortifying
wall yards thick, engraven on one side with the emblem of the
old British East India Company and on the other with the
Dutch arms, to emerge at a modern wharf scurrying with people
unloading goods from, say, a Japanese freighter. On the roads
you will pass Sinhalese in neat business suits as well as the old-
fashioned men who still prefer sarongs, and grow their hair long
and hold it in place with a circular comb. In the little side
streets you are certain to come upon the dark caves of shops where
workmen are polishing gems, for Galle has been famous for
precious and semiprecious stones since the days when King
Solomon is supposed to have sent to Galle for jewels for the
Queen of Sheba.

A jeweler once remarked that any visitor who thought seriously
of investing a large amount of money in gems should learn by
heart the first two lines of the poem, "Twinkle, twinkle, little

star, How I wonder what you are," and I suppose if you are interested in buying the perfect star sapphires and star rubies for which Ceylon is most celebrated, then you should have expert advice or deal only with the established and reputable jewelers (any of the Ceylonese government tourist bureaus will help you with this as with so much else in Ceylon). But far more fun, particularly if you haven't too much money to spend, is to find your way to the tiny stalls and workshops, to see the men cutting tortoiseshell into decorative combs and boxes, or to watch the green and orange fire of an opal come to life under the polishing stone. You can buy a package of opal chips (two hundred for about ten dollars) and put your sense of fantasy to work in designing necklaces or bracelets for yourself, and have the pleasure of seeing your ideas take shape, for you can get jewelry quickly and reasonably set in Galle.

Any evening as you sit on the grass-grown ramparts and watch the sunset, a number of jewel vendors are certain to come by, to crouch beside you if you want and spread their merchandise out on the ground. They will show you some of the favorite Sinhalese designs—scorpion pins set with milky moonstones, or the most popular local necklace, a moonstone choker with short trembling tassels of moonstones hanging from it. They may have some of the beautiful antique hairpins that some of the older women still wear—a tapering spear of silver or gold, with a brilliant cluster of jewels at one end; sometimes these are Matara diamonds (white zircons) and occasionally they are a wild, glittering mixture of real diamonds, rubies, emeralds and sapphires. The vendors will always show you as well packages of unset stones—pink and green tourmalines, the lovely smoky Ceylon topazes, amethysts from the local mines, the blinding shine of white sapphires and water sapphires—and since the prices range from twenty-five cents to twenty-five dollars, you can amuse yourself for hours indulging your more frivolous fancies in jewels.

The new town of Galle is separated from the old fort by a wide green. Beyond it the new shops and markets are strung along the edge of the bay, and smaller compounds and residential sections branch off inland. This is where the town's liveliest activity is concentrated. On festival days music blares out from the shops, and the crowded square in the center of town blossoms with lights and papier mâché decorations and plaster figures of Lord Buddha. Strings of paper stars and streamers are stretched from roof to roof across the road, and the children tear about in false faces, with butterflies in their hair. At Wesak, for instance, an impromptu shrine was set up and next to it a bamboo pavilion restaurant where dozens of devout Buddhists worked for hours preparing rice and vegetables to feed the priests and pilgrims as an act of merit.

Even on ordinary days you will often see a band of small boys in tinsel-covered costumes raising money for some temple by singing and dancing on the street and collecting the coppers that people give them. But the most exciting aspect of local life for a foreigner to see is a devil dance. There is a devil dance going on somewhere nearby almost every week, and nobody objects if you go and watch it. If by any chance the devils of the district don't seem to be much in evidence when you are there, you can always arrange a devil dance of your own—preferably in a neighboring village where the atmosphere will not be strangely mixed, as it is in town, with dimly heard music from a next-door radio, or the electric gleam of street lights. By the light of blazing palm-leaf torches in a village clearing the dancers perform the astonishing spins and acrobatics, rub themselves with red-hot

embers, fling gunpowder on their torches to make sudden sheets
of flame, and late in the evening enact the terrifying dances
of the eighteen demons in green, scarlet and black masks and
weird costumes made of thick leaves.

If you ask a Sinhalese just what the meaning of the devil
dance is, he is apt to reply vaguely that it is "auspicious," or
that it "frightens away the devils." If you insist, as I once did,
"But how do you decide when to have a devil dance?" you may
get the reply that was offered to me, "Well, you just *know*."

"But *how* do you know?"

"If you've had several misfortunes in your house that are the
work of devils or witchcraft, you can have a devil dance to purify
the house."

"But how do you know it's devils and not just coincidence?"

"Oh, you always know. And then there are certain diseases
that can only be cured by a devil dance."

"Influenza, for instance?"

"Oh no."

"Appendicitis? Dysentery? High blood pressure?"

"No, no. Not that kind. You recognize the disease at once; it
affects the mind." After a moment's thoughtful pause he added
his own question, "You've been in America; tell me, what do
Americans do when they have demons?"

You can see devil dances just about anywhere in Ceylon, but
the ones around Galle are particularly good because some of the
best dancing families live in nearby villages. In a small town a
few miles from Galle you can see another of the special and exhilarating traditional performances of Ceylon—the great masked
plays and dances known as Kolam which have vanished from the
rest of the island. In Ambalangoda two companies of players
still put on the long mythological stories and satires, and the

actors appear in huge painted wooden masks carved a century ago, some of them so heavy that a couple of the characters—the king and queen, for instance—can only be on stage for a couple of minutes at a time and can do nothing more strenuous than walk slowly around in a circle before the attendants rush to help them take off the masks and allow them to rest.

But of all the exciting things to do and beautiful things to see, I think I shall remember with most pleasure those tropical-paradise aspects of the island which so impressed me the day I arrived, and which now seem to me focused on Galle and the magnificent coast that stretches away on each side of the town. The lazy days on any of the many beaches, with Sinhalese children doing tricks in the water or catching small fish in the rock pools to amuse you, the sails of the fishing boats far out to sea, and the men on perilous-looking stilts fishing in the surf, the bright water and the coconut palms. The cool evenings as you have a drink on the ramparts high above the ocean, or sit with friends under the huge umbrellas of the rain trees in front of the hotel, occasionally bargaining idly with the women who bring round baskets of hand-made lace or the jewel vendors, or simply staring out across the lovely arc of the bay of Galle and watching the lights come on in the town.

{ INDEX }

aboriginal tribes, 5
acacia trees, Cambodia, 72
adat, Balinese, 171
Agung, Chokorda, 169, 172-173,
    179-180, 183-184
alcohol, 62
alus, 15
Ambalangoda, Ceylon, 222-223
American automobiles and goods,
    Thailand, 124
American influence, Philippine
    Is., 41, 44
Americans, massacre of, by Mos-
    lems, Philippines, 32
amok, tradition of, in Philippines,
    7
Ananda pagoda, Burma, 198
ancient religions, evidences of, 8
Andaman Is., 12
Angkor, Cambodia, 3, 16, 78-79
Angkor-Thom, 83
Angkor Vat, temple of, 81-82
Annam, 60, 80, 96
    meaning of name, 10
anticolonial fighting, post-World
    War II, 14
Anuradhapura, Ceylon, 215
Aran Paknam, Thailand, 111

Arc en Ciel night club, Vietnam,
    62
architecture, SE Asia, 16
areca nut, 89, 188
Asoka, ruler of Maurya empire,
    11, 214
ato, 30
Australia, 158
Ayudhya, Thailand, 116

balance of power, vs. mutual un-
    derstanding, 23
Bali, 3, 140, 163-184
    absence of compliments in,
        170
    artistry, 181
    beauty of countryside, 168
    cock fighting, 177
    cremation, 183
    Dutch invasion of, 182
    ease of divorce, 178
    foreigners' enthusiasm for,
        157
    Hinduism, 7
    as idyllic island, 16
    legong music, 180

227

233